Success ... In 10 Steps!
Home Business Warning:
Don't Get Toasted Like a Pop-Tart!

By Michael Dlouhy

We believe in you

Michael Dlouhy
2012

Cover design by Peter Giordano
Email: peterg@theghostwriter.com

1

This book is dedicated to …

My wife and soulmate Linda: your inspiration, your belief, your encouragement and your work have made it all possible;

My son Matthew: you're the best son a father could ask for AND you taught me how to check email(!);

My daughter Amanda: for all the love and support you've given me;

My business partners, Dave Cones, Richard Dennis, and Michael Anderson: your efforts have made the team a success; and

All the Success Team Builders: you have applied the information in the real world, given us your feedback, and you have worked hard to achieve your dreams.

I truly love and appreciate all of you!

Success In 10 Steps
"Home Business Warning: Don't Get Toasted Like a Pop-Tart!"

Introduction
No Good Deed Goes Unpunished, Parts 1 & 2

1. Bottom-Fishing For Heavy Hitters
- What Do Your Past & Jimmy Hoffa Have In Common? (This one is SO Obvious!)
- **You Sometimes Think YOU Are Nuts? Heck ... I Joined 100 MLMs!**
- I Never Realized There Was So Much Stuff I Didn't Want
- **And the Lambs Shall Lie Down With The Lions (Cover your eyes to avoid blood spatters.)**
- How They Rob You Under The Radar
- **Bad Blood In Big Companies**
- **Oh, The Questions I Hear!**
- Network Marketing Deviltry
- **Why You Should Never Wrestle a Pig**
- Breast Stroking Across The English Channel
- **The Monk In The White Lab Coat**
- Voodoo MLM Economics
- **Network Marketing Angels ... Whoops! Doggoneit! It's Still More Devils**
- The Stupidest Lie They ALL Tell You!
- **Marketing Insanity**
- Even Your Mirror Lies!
- **Opportunity Comes On Little Cat's Feet (Scams use a sledgehammer.)**
- What The Heck Is Pentacle Leadership?
- **Hannibal Lecter Missed His Calling**
- Her Ranch Was The Size of Rhode Island

3

2. "Look Deep Deep DEEP Into My Eyes!"

🏃 Your Business Life Expectancy Is About 45 Minutes

🏃 **Your Warm Market Has Ice In Their Veins**

🏃 How To Get Staying Power

🏃 **Let's Play Sherlock Holmes**

🏃 **Shocking - The Family Member I Am Driven To Get Even With!**

🏃 Go Catch Some Cannonballs, Boy!

🏃 **Your Brain Ain't Worth Dog Meat (no offense, Fido)**

🏃 Get Serious!

🏃 **Some People Wear Me Out**

🏃 Is YOUR Biscuit Cooked?

3. A BIG Research Surprise

🏃 Opportunity Wears a Fake Nose & Mustache

🏃 **Rabbit's Foot, Anyone?**

🏃 How To Catch Flies

🏃 **Give Your Prospects a Puppy**

🏃 **The Man Who Stared Down IBM**

🏃 Your Best, Cheapest Solution

🏃 **The Bad News**

🏃 The Good News

🏃 **"Heart" Decisions vs. "Head" Decisions**

4. Get "Down 'n Dirty" in MLM

🏃 Network Marketing Is NOT What They Tell You

🏃 **The Knife In The Heart**

🏃 Have Some WD-40 On That Steak?

🏃 Two Ways To Stop Your NEXT Spouse From Demanding a Pre-Nup

🏃 **1978 – The Word Picture That Turned My Life Upside Down**

🏃 The REAL Truth About Network Marketing

4

8. Pay Dirt! Get And Keep Your People

🏃 OK. I'm Not Tom Cruise. But I'm Not Elmer Fudd, Either ...

🏃 **The Dark Side of MLM**

🏃 So What?

9. How To Evaluate An Opportunity

🏃 Your Ex-Spouse Was An Optimist

🏃 **It Just SEEMS Like Brain Surgery**

🏃 Best of BOTH Worlds

🏃 **Last One In Is a Rotten Egg**

🏃 Never Dedicate Your Life To An Inanimate Object

🏃 **A Whole Lotta Connivin' Goin' On**

🏃 Opportunity Hides In The Tall Grass

10. Focus Until Your Eyes Cross

🏃 Multiple Streams of Outgo

🏃 **Assaulted Right & Left**

🏃 **How To Send Prospects Racing for the Exit**

🏃 **Go Ahead – Argue With Me!**

🏃 How One Famous Company Drove Their Customers Away

🏃 Ambushed By Human Nature & Common Sense

🏃 **What Your Prospects Believe**

🏃 The Sun, The Moon, The Stars, The Universe, & Your Prospect's Head

🏃 **To Thine Own Self Be True**

🏃 I'll Get In Your Head & Under Your Skin

🏃 **Let's Get Illogical!**

🏃 Never Underestimate The Cost of Logic

🏃 A Series of Harmless Decisions? HAH!

🏃 Yum, Yum, Yum!

Introduction

No Good Deed Goes Unpunished: Part 1

Listen carefully.

I'm well aware your intentions were gallant: to provide for your family all the things YOU never had, to spend more quality time with them, to help others like yourself grow & prosper.

And remember what happened next?

You were lied to. You were "leveraged". The Heavy Hitters used you for batting practice. You got thrown in the muck, untrained, unprepared. Your checking account was drained. Your credit cards were maxed out. Friends & relatives screened your phone calls.

Then you looked in the mirror and called yourself, "Loser!"

I know, I know.

It started because you want the same things I wanted.

You want to be your own boss, answer to no one … and earn a good living doing it. You want to go where you want, when you want. You want to spend $200 on dinner without batting an eye.

You want precious time NOW with those you love. You want the money & freedom to take a day off – or 2 weeks off – and maybe fly to some faraway island on a whim.

You want to work and socialize with people you like & admire, who share your outlook on life and your goals. You want the self-satisfaction of achieving your goals, and the self-fulfillment of helping others reach theirs. You want financial independence.

You DON'T want more rejection. You DON'T want to have to sell anything to anyone. And you sure DON'T want another MLM.

Good stuff. Holy mackerel, sounds just like ME!

So here I am. I have no choice but to write this book. Truly, no control. You'll read why in Chapter 2.

But here's what I do control: This book is free. No company is mentioned or promoted. No opportunity is mentioned or promoted.

You'll find 20 tons of ebooks all over the internet, full of affiliate links. Trust them at your peril, because they profit on every recommendation they make.

My purpose is to share what I've learned in nearly 30 years in network marketing, and present a 10-step success plan you can use with ANY network marketing opportunity.

The plan is NOT easy. But it's simple.

It's NOT "I'll do all the work FOR you." It only works if YOU do.

It's NOT "get-rich-quick." But you can create a lifetime residual income.

What's in it for me, you ask? That question is answered in Chapters 2 & 5. Don't worry. Helping you helps me. It's part of my giving back to this great industry.

I wish you the absolute best, and I hope you use this information. It could change your life.

Are you game? Then read on!

No Good Deed Goes Unpunished, Part 2

People ask me:
- *"Your e-book is great! Why on earth do you give it away free?"*
- *"Your telephone training is great! Why is it free?"*
- *"Your 'Colors' CD is great! Why is it so cheap?"*
- *"Why do you help me for free when I'm not in your company?"*
- *... and a dozen other variations.*

In the early 1990s, I joined over 100 MLM opportunities. I tracked, cataloged, analyzed & evaluated EVERYTHING they did: products, compensation plans, marketing, distributor support, profitability, etc.

The Ugly Results

I'm a fun-loving, easy-going guy. But my teeth clenched and my fingers curled into fists of rage. **I was stunned by how many companies and "Heavy Hitters" make HUGE profits NOT on product sales, but instead by selling a ton of worthless marketing materials to the distributors who trust and believe in them!**

I get mad just thinking about it. This is why you find widespread cynicism & skepticism amongst network marketers.

I can't blame them.

But you should hear the calls I get from people trying to figure out how I'm going to bamboozle them.

First, they figure I'm trying to steal their people.

Fact is, they don't HAVE any people. None who trust them, anyway. Many uplines' idea of support is to tell you the lies we'll cover in Chapter 1.
TRUE support is to take you by the hand and lead you through every step of this business, so you can actually experience it in real time and get good at it. THAT is what we do on our phone calls.

No company is ever mentioned on those calls. No product is mentioned. No one is ever recruited.

Some people figure our calls must be rigged so anybody who calls gets billed on their phone bill!

Listen. Our MLM business brings good income, thank you. Our tools & phone calls support our people. And they work their butts off. And Linda & I love them and appreciate them.

We owe everything to this business. It tortures me to hear people denigrate network marketing because of the greed of some companies and their "Super Star Reps."

I don't do ANYTHING in life that isn't fun. Whatever I do, it's because I love it.

So I do what I can to balance the scales. I choose to support with every fiber of my body ANYONE who invests their hopes & dreams & life into this industry. It makes my day to help keep their spark alive.

I will train anyone for free. No strings. I am not threatened by anyone or any company in this industry.

But I understand that they are threatened by me. Most STILL don't take the time and make the commitment to train their own people.

Still Skeptical? I get the skepticism. Really. But enough is enough. Get over it. If you want to live your life distrusting everybody, then your life is pretty much over, anyway. Goodbye, good luck. Don't let the door hit you in your butt on the way out.

For everyone else: Let's get started!

Sincerely,

Michael Dlouhy

#1
Bottom-
Fishing
For
Heavy
Hitters

What Do Your Past &
Jimmy Hoffa Have In Common?

Yes. Sure. Absolutely. The answer is obvious.

They're both dead.

However, it's a bit of a trick question, too.

Why?

Well, I personally don't know if Jimmy Hoffa is part of the foundation of Giants Stadium in New Jersey, or if he's buried in a backyard in Detroit. But I'll tell you this: Jimmy Hoffa IS dead. I know he's dead. You know he's dead. Jimmy Hoffa knows he's dead.

Your past, on the other hand ... well, I know it's dead. You know it's dead. Right?

Or are you like most people, reliving your business failures every day of your life?

If so, you've come to the right place.

You Sometimes Think YOU Are Nuts?
Heck ... I Joined 100 MLM Opportunities!

Almost 20 years ago, we joined a 1-year-old wellness MLM that is still going strong today. Our timing was mostly luck, but it was perfect. We used what we knew at the time and built a very lucrative business, and helped others do the same.

By 1991, our residual income was large enough that we had no financial needs. So I decided to totally focus on learning everything I could about network marketing & MLM.

So I joined every network marketing company I could find ... probably a hundred or more. I don't know how many $30 or $50 or $100 binders I bought in a 3-year period, but it was a ton. I'd join, buy their kit, try some of their products, get on their conference calls, look at everything they did, & listen to everything they said.

I Never Realized There Was So
Much Stuff I Didn't Want!

I spent many, many, many late nights cataloging it, studying it, analyzing it all, figuring out why one worked and another didn't. Or why some would work awhile and then stop.

I was amazed at how many companies talked a great product talk, but their profit center was NOT products!

And The Lambs Shall Lie Down With The
Lions (Cover your eyes to avoid blood spatters.)

Their focus was selling distributor kits and brochures & books & audiotapes & videotapes to their distributors. Many

13

distributors would buy 100s or even 1000s of tapes at a time to use in mailings. Even in quantity, some of these companies charged reps $2 or $3 each for tapes that cost 20¢ to duplicate!

They were making a killing on the backs of their reps!

And with all these companies, it always came back to the same fundamental principles.

Bad Blood In Big Companies

They failed for the same reason. Most of the companies or large organizations I've seen crash & burn, it happened because of greed & ego.

Greed & ego.

Other companies did it right. They had good sponsoring systems in place, and they sold their promotional material at a reasonable price.

> **Success leaves footprints in the sand that you can follow. If you can't follow the footprints, you must be on the wrong beach.**

Oh, The Questions I Hear!

I've talked with thousands of people in the network marketing business. They ask themselves certain questions. Maybe some are familiar to you:

- Why am I not smart enough to do this business?

- Why am I successful in corporate America and fail in network marketing?

- Why does the phone weigh so much?

- Why do the "No"s hurt so bad?

- Am I too tall? Am I too short?

- **I worked so hard and still can't do it. What's wrong with me? What's wrong with the company? What's wrong with the product?**

- The Hitters tell me, "If it is to be, it's up to me." Other people do this. Why can't I?

- Why do these companies fail me?

- Why did the federal government shut my company down?

- I maxed out my credit card on advertising. Why did it NOT work?

- **I went to the meetings. I did three-way phone calls. Why doesn't everyone see this?**

- Why don't they have the literature in Spanish?

- Where's the teamwork?

- Why isn't this fun?

- Where are the facts and figures?

- Where's the money?

Network Marketing Deviltry

It's not your fault.

Let that sink in. How does that make you feel?

I don't care what any heavy hitter has ever told you. Fact is they've lied to you. Doesn't that make you angry?

I can PROVE the cards are stacked against you. That's why it's not your fault.

Why You Should Never Wrestle a Pig

Why? Because you'll both get dirty, and the pig likes it. That's the best advice you'll get about hitching your wagon to an MLM Heavy Hitter.

If this makes good business common sense to you, stick around. If not, click that "X" in the upper right-hand corner. Nobody will know, except you.

Breast Stroking Across The English Channel

Can you swim?

You can?

Great.

Can you swim across a small pond?

Maybe?

OK.

How about the same small frozen pond in Maine in January?

Oh, really? Why not?

OK, how about the English Channel in July? (It's not frozen.)

**What do you mean, "No"? I thought
you said you could swim!**

Other people have done it. What do you mean, "Too hard, too far, you haven't been trained"? Those are just excuses.

OK, OK. We'll get you a coach, a mentor. He's a GREAT guy. Great swimmer, too. I saw him do 6 laps in the pool one day. He'll work with you all week. THEN we'll dump you out in the Channel.

What do you mean, "NO!"

Kind of like getting marriage counseling from someone who's never been married, isn't it? I've been married 33 years. If I wanted advice, I'd talk to someone who's been married 50 years. Not 2 years. Not "read a book about it."

OK, let's get to the first lie. (And if you've heard me say some of this before, that's OK. The more you hear it, the easier it'll be for you to start new with a clean slate.)

The Monk In The White Lab Coat

The Hitters tell you network marketing is a sales business.

It's not.

Truth: Network marketing is a teaching & mentoring business. If you study vitamins, or long-distance switches, or the age of the monk in the white lab coat that scraped the mold off the rock on the full moon twice a year ... or ANY product or service ... you're wasting your time.

Your product is people. So study people. Find out how you can help them reach their dreams.

THEIR dreams. Not your dreams.

People join people. They don't join companies. People don't care that the president of your company is a family man and has 3 or 4 families to prove it.

Build people. People will build the business.

When you build people, your retention rate goes through the roof.

Voodoo MLM Economics

Companies say, "We Keep 93% of Our People!"

They lie.

Truth: There was a phone company a few years back that had to publicize their retention rate, because they were publicly traded.

Take a guess. Out of every 100 people they signed up, how many were still in the business a year later?

50%? HAH!

25%? As they say in the Hertz commercial, "Not exactly!"

10%? You're getting warm ...

The public record showed 6% to 7% retention. That's not 67% ... it's 6 to 7% retention. So you build your business for a year, you buy advertising, you do 3-way calls, you go to meetings, you talk to all your friends & relatives, and you wind up recruiting 100 people! Yippee! You're almost rich.

Well, not exactly. Why? Because what you have left is 6 to 7 people out of 100 (!) still building the business.

Ooops ... wait ... that's not all you've got. You also have smashed dreams, maxed-out credit cards, and probably a LARGE bunch of people who hide when they see you coming.

Whatever you do in network marketing must be duplicatable for the masses. Six to 7% retention is not smart business.

That brings up the next big lie.

Network Marketing Angels...Whoops! Doggone it! It's STILL More Devils!

The Hitters tell you, "It's Just A Numbers Game."

Truth: People are people - not numbers. They have goals, dreams and desires. They are mothers, fathers, sisters, brothers, aunts, uncles, nieces, nephews, grandmothers, and grandfather's to someone that loves them. They are not a number, but real people.

If you treat them like a number, I promise you: you have NO future in network marketing.

This lie teaches people to be a recruiter, not a sponsor. Recruit, recruit, recruit. Numbers, numbers, numbers. Lies, lies, lies.

A recruiter never knows their personally sponsored people's "WHY." Or their dreams, goals, or spouse's or children's names. It's only about numbers.

To succeed long-term, you need to become a mentor with a servant's heart. When you do, people will ask you to PLEASE sponsor them into your business.

Ever wonder why you get so many "NO"s? Take a look at ...

The Stupidest Lie They ALL Tell You!

The Heavy Hitters tell you "NO" is a good thing!

Go get 100 "NO's", they say. You're just getting closer to a "YES."

THIS baby is REALLY one of my favorites!

Isn't it the stupidest thing you ever heard? What nitwit came up with this idea? The word "NO" has taken more good people out of this industry that any other word in the English language.

Picture this: all day long you've been flirting with your spouse. At night you take a bath, candles around the tub, soft music, perfect for romance. Some hugging, some kissing.

And your spouse says "NO!"

GREAT! Just 99 more "NO"s and you'll get lucky!

And some nitwit says NO is a good thing.

Onward.

Marketing Insanity

The Hitters have more wonderful advice for you: "Talk to EVERYBODY about your business opportunity."

Oh, man, don't get me started!

There's an old saying you hear from time to time: the reason you have 2 ears and 1 mouth is you should LISTEN twice as much as you TALK.

Take a good look next time you see a Heavy Hitter. I swear, if you look closely, you'll see the guy has zero ears and THREE MOUTHS!

OK. For the sake of argument, let's see where their advice leads us.

Let's say you owned a shoe store. You get 300 visitors. If you have the right styles, colors, & price, could you sell some shoes? Absolutely.

But you'd never try fitting a corporate Secretary working at the Trump Towers with men's construction work boots. Not appropriate.

And not everyone wants your business opportunity.

This advice works great for the **10%** of the population who are salespeople (more on this in Chapter 5).

But if you're part of the 90% who hate pushy, aggressive people, THIS lie will make you feel totally inadequate to ever build a networking business.

The key is target marketing. Just talk to people who want your products and services. Lead with benefits so REAL prospects see the value your offer and ask you for more information.

Even Your Mirror Lies!

The Hitters give you self-talk to use when you look in the mirror: "If It Is To Be, It's Up To Me."

No skyscraper or successful network marketing organization has ever been built by one person. It takes teamwork, people from every walk of life & experience level coming together, working together. It takes hundreds, often thousands of people working for one common goal, to build the skyscraper or the network marketing organization.

Consider:

- No steel mill worker = no steel = no building.
- No glassmaker = no windows = no building.
- No makers of carpet, tile, marble, lumber, air-conditioning, drywall, concrete, paint, shingles, plumbing fixtures, electrical wiring, tar paper, drywall compound, elevators, mortar, bricks, paint brush, doors, crown molding, wallpaper, nails, screws, lights, cabinets, etc. = no skyscraper.

You absolutely need a great product. You won't sustain success without one. But like the skyscraper, the MOST critical is a LOT of people working together.

I have observed and analyzed a TON of network marketing businesses over the last 26 years. And you know what?

Every single one of them that was NOT people-&-relationship-driven, no matter how good its products or services, no matter how well-managed, has either gone broke or struggled to keep its head above water.

And every "relationship-driven" business, no matter how inferior its products or services and no matter how poorly-managed, was successful almost without fail.

Now ... companies with low quality products or services WILL ultimately fail. But MLM companies or groups with wonderful products & services - but who stress "numbers game, recruit, recruit, recruit" - will never scratch the surface of their potential.

Obviously, the biggest successes are people-and-relationship-driven companies with good products or services & good management.

Bottom line? Get a good product or service to sell. THEN focus on helping OTHER people reach their dreams. THAT is your top priority.

Opportunity Comes On Little Cat's Feet (Scams use a sledgehammer.)

When you get some website that boasts of the millions they've earned or some email that yells at you to ACT NOW!!! or some guy on the phone who corners you with a closing question that only a total loser could ever answer "No" to, ask yourself:

Is this duplicatable? Could I ever do this? Could I train all my people to do this?

It's obvious, isn't it? If you only ever respond to approaches that you would be comfortable using yourself, and that you could train others to use, then you will automatically avoid most scams.

What the Heck Is Pentacle Leadership?

You need solid Pentacle Leadership for success. Find a mentor. You must have a mentor to be a mentor. You want a mastermind group of like-minded people who want YOU to succeed. You want up-line support available when you need it.

Pentacle leadership means Michael mentoring Dave, Dave mentoring Laura, Laura mentoring Scott, Scott mentoring Cheryl, Cheryl mentoring Roisann, Roisann mentoring Judith and the people that Judith will mentor is endless. THIS type of leadership creates your mastermind group.

Want to make a million dollars?

Mastermind with millionaires.

If you want to make $30,000 a year, then mastermind with people who make $30,000 a year.

Consider this VERY carefully: For most people, their yearly income is the average of their 5 closest friends.

Do YOUR 5 closest friends have what you want? If not, why would you EVER listen to their opinions on business?

Say you want to invest in real estate. Would you ask the person who rents a home? Or the person with 27 homes, 16 townhouses, 2 farms, one in Oklahoma, one in Texas, and 27 commercial properties?

To build a business, why on earth would you listen to people who've never done it? You've got to evaluate who you take advice from.

Want success? Then you'd better get your action plan from successful people.

One last lie ... last, but certainly not least:

Hannibal Lecter Missed His Calling

Instead of filleting HIS friends and enjoying them with a fine chianti, as he did in *"Silence of the Lambs,"* Hannibal might have achieved the same satisfaction as a Heavy Hitter.

He'd have said, "Hey! I made 4 million dollars last year. I'll help you get rich. Come on up to my place, and I'll show you how I did it!"

Do you know there is a coaching company or university that charges you thousands of dollars for coaching ...

... and the owner of that Company has NEVER built a downline in any network marketing company? They tell you your personal coach is full time in network marketing. You better ask to see their 1099s.

The president of that Company openly admits he cannot stand network marketing companies.

This last lie should make you madder than all the others.

In fact, YOU should ask ME: "Hey, Michael! Where's YOUR coaching certificate?"

Well, 26 years in the real world of Network Marketing is my certificate. I have the battle scars all over my mind and body to prove it.

People also ask, "Why don't you charge for your coaching?"

We'll talk about that in the next chapter. It's personal … but I'll reveal my exact reasons.

Remember greed and ego? Focus on the money and you'll always chase money. Our goal is to help teach, train and mentor people on how to "Become A Mentor With A Servant's Heart."

And it seems to work OK financially, too.

Her Ranch Was The Size of Rhode Island

A few years ago I got a phone call from a lady in Texas. Sometime earlier, she had started a major corporation, whose name you know. It probably had a branch in your town. It's since been bought out by an even bigger fish.

Anyway, this lady was very gracious. She was going to start an MLM company, and she wanted feedback from some MLM leaders on what she was doing. She flew Linda & me to what must have been the biggest ranch in all of Texas.

We were there 3 days, along with several MLM "Heavy Hitters".

She showed us her products and she showed us her compensation plan, and she asked for our thoughts.

The Big Boys (and Girls) were flabbergasted by her wonderful products and astonished by her compensation plan. They told her she had a HUGE winner.

Every single one of them wanted her to build the company under them.

When my turn came, I told her the truth: she was dead in the water. She had a bunch of "me-too" products. And her compensation plan was from the dark ages of MLM, piling up money for the leaders and sacrificing all the part-timers who would hope to fulfill their lifelong dream of having their own business.

With this comp plan, the part-timers were destined to fail. They'd never understand why. They would blame themselves, and many would never take the risk again.

Dora (not her real name) pulled me aside before we left and thanked me. Somehow, despite all the smoke coming from the Heavy Hitters, she knew Truth when she heard it.

She stuck to the business she knew.

But if the Heavy Hitters would try pulling that bullcrap with one of the richest women in the country, imagine what they'd figure they could put over on YOU!

#2
"Look Deep, Deep, DEEP Into My Eyes!"

Your Business Life Expectancy Is About 45 Minutes

OK. You nailed me. That's an exaggeration.

But not by a lot.

Ninety percent of new businesses fail the first year.

And 90% of the rest fail in the next 4 years.

THAT is tough.

You're excited. You start. A thousand things go wrong. You want to quit a thousand times.

Most people just quit.

**You need a strong enough reason to do it.
Then if WHAT you're doing doesn't work,
you'll figure out some other way. But if
you're at all wishy-washy, you're a goner.**

First thing we do in coaching is help you figure out your
"WHY".

Your Warm Market Has Ice In Their Veins

A nailed "WHY" can save your life.

Most people have a huge problem when they decide to
improve their situation in life. That problem is one or more of
the people closest to you will NOT want to see you succeed.

This is a FACT for virtually everyone on this planet, and you
are no different. You can argue with me until you're blue in
the face, but that won't change anything.

**There are people in your life who will be threatened when
you make a passionate push to success. They will complain
and criticize and try to suck the life out of you.**

Why? Because THEIR life is a mess and misery truly does
love company.

Your best option is to get rid of them. Next best is to have an
AMAZING "WHY", a 99.9% "WHY", that will keep you
going through rain, sleet, snow, flood, pestilence, nuclear
holocaust, or the criticism of a "loved" one.

So why is it critical you do THIS business? And why is it
critical that you succeed?

How To Get "Staying Power"

People always tell their goals.

Fine. You need goals.

But your "WHY" is a big, big, big reason that will keep you going.

Where's your fire? What do you LOVE? What do you HATE? What is REALLY important to you? What do you REALLY want? What situation in life do you want to get out of so it never ever, EVER happens again?

It's not goals. It's not money, either.

When I started coaching, people would write their "WHY"... usually money. They'd need to pay a big hospital bill, or replace a car. Whatever.

But your real "WHY" is never money.
It's about who YOU really are.
Your driving factor must be WAY more than money.

It's something you want ... or something you want to get away from. Better yet, BOTH. If your "WHY" is a 70% and you come up against an obstacle that's a 72%, you're gone. You'll drop out, disappear.

But when your "WHY" is a 99.9%, then you're here to stay and be successful.

Why are you on this planet? In one form or another, you're here to change lives, touch lives, and help people. What were you meant to do?

Let's Play Sherlock Holmes

A new business is always a risk. People risk to avoid pain, or to achieve pleasure. **Answering these questions may help you find your "WHY".**

- What gets you REALLY excited?
- How many hours a week do you work?
- What do you LOVE about your job?
- What do you HATE about your job?
- What do you do with your free time?
- If you had 2 months vacation and all the money you wanted, what would you do?
- How do you like the people you work with?
- What problem scares you to death that more money could solve?
- What do you just absolutely HATE about your life that more money could solve?
- If you had all the money you needed, what HUGE problem would go away?
- If you had all the TIME in the world to do anything you wanted, what would you do?
- Other than money, what are you looking for?

I'll give you a starting point.

The #1 reason I am in this business, that I'm here on this planet, is because I LOVE my family. I want to spend more quality time with each of them. People say, "Michael, that's nuts. You work full-time in network marketing, you work at home. You're already right there."

Yes. BUT ... I treat business as business. When I'm in the office, I'm in the office. Same as if my office was 20 miles away.

31

But that lets me have that time I cherish with my wife Linda, my son Matthew, and my daughter Amanda.

I realize that many husbands and fathers rarely or never get the chance to do the things they want with their families because of the demands on their time from simply earning a living. Or, they don't have the money.

For me, the rewards of MLM have allowed me to build the relationships I cherish.

Linda & I talk a LOT. It may be serious business conversation when we're out to dinner, or simple, crazy, "laugh-to-tears" talks late at night. We love to drive on the beach at Daytona, or go snorkeling at Looe Key.

Matthew & I ride motorcycles & go scuba diving. We talk about business & computers, engines & race cars. Sometimes he even wants advice!

Amanda has a T Top Camero with a "scoop" on the hood. I taught her how to change her oil & service it. We have long talks in the boat out on the water or after watching a movie together. I love to hug her at the end of the day.

Life is good when you get to do the things that make life really worthwhile.

Shocking - The Family Member I Am Driven to Get Even With!

#2, my second "WHY", is to feel good about myself.

This one's very personal ... just as your "WHY" should be.

My mother was a pessimist. She'd tell me, "You're no good. You'll never amount to anything. You'll never have a pot to pee in."

But I programmed my mind to reject what she told me.

My father's sister, my Aunt Honey, would say, "Michael, I love you. I'm proud of you. You can do anything you want. Look at that beautiful picture you drew for me!"

At 5 years old, I made a conscious decision that I liked my Aunt's reality better than I liked my mother's reality.

So when my mother started running me down, I'd just step into the theater of my mind. I'd picture & hear my Aunt Honey saying what a great kid I was. I'd literally feel her hugging me. I'd stop feeling bad.

And now, to feel good about myself, I need to be "Aunt Honey." I MUST help people.

Go Catch Some Cannonballs, Boy!

In WWII, US soldiers took the "dog tags" from the necks of their fallen brothers, to track who didn't make it. General George Patton used to calculate how many dog tags it would take to win a particular battle.

Now … preserving freedom for your children, your family, your neighbors, your countrymen … THAT is worth the ultimate sacrifice.

But when you start a networking business, they line up to take your dog tag. Raise your hand if you're ready to give your life to increase some general's income.

The generals send YOU to the front line to catch the cannonballs. They hope you'll get a few orders before you get blown to smithereens and they have to replace you.

Now, generals get paid pretty good. But after awhile, if you have any sense of humanity, all those dead bodies begin to bother you.

That's why we've done mentoring for free for people in ANY network marketing company for more years than I can remember. We've never charged a dime.

My credentials? Twenty-six years of hard knocks, 26 years of life lessons. Full-time in network marketing since 1991.

I have scars all over my body, head to toe, from life experiences in network marketing.

I've seen it all. Every time a company or distributorship explodes and goes away, it's because of greed and ego. Beware greed & ego. Stay away.

The people we attract don't have a greed & ego problem. They are humble people, people who want success.

Your Brain Ain't Worth Dog Meat (No offense, Fido)

There's a husband and wife team that was with a network marketing company for 2 years and never sponsored anybody. We've been coaching them 7 or 8 months. It's amazing. They may win the top recruiter award in their company this year. They're sponsoring 10 or 12 people a month.

They've gone from their heads to their hearts.

You'll hear me say this a lot. Network marketing is NOT a sales business. It's certainly not a thinking business.

It's a LISTENING business. It's a TEACHING/MENTORING business. This husband & wife aren't selling anything. That's not just a line. Really, they're NOT selling anything. Today, they are reaching their hearts out to others who need help.

They are mentoring for free.

I exist to mentor & coach you to success. Not MY success. YOURS! Your success is a beautiful thing to me. If I can help you create success, then my future takes care of itself.

So my first bit of coaching is, figure out your own "WHY". Write it down. Test it mentally. (Will it keep you going in VERY tough times?)

More tips to help you pinpoint your "WHY":

- What does your family mean to you?
- What do you want for your own personal growth?
- What you want to accomplish in your lifetime?
- What scares you to death?
- What would it mean to you to help others change their lives?
- What really excites you in life?
- What REALLY makes you angry about your life?
- What would you like to give the people you love most?
- What really, really gets you emotional?

Get Serious – Find Your Why!

It's critical. You need a strong, written "WHY", to stick around long enough to be successful in this business.

Listen to me. Listen to me. **Listen to me!!!!!!**

Maybe I'm just weird. But to me, there is NOTHING in this business more fun and emotionally stimulating and satisfying than to poke around the dark recesses of your psyche, spot old frustrations and vengefulness and crazed hatreds and lustful desires and unfulfilled dreams and long-time, unachieved goals and all that other wonderful stuff that makes us who we are …

… and then HARNESS it all to help you achieve what you most want in life!

Look. You've been the EFFECT of this stuff long enough. Now it's time to turn it around and USE IT!

In fact, a nailed "WHY" is SO powerful, and I have seen it work so BIG so many times, that I am absolutely unable to stop myself from helping you find exactly the "WHY" that drives YOU.

WOW! I get REALLY excited when I dig into THIS stuff!

So when you're happy with your "WHY", email it to the person who gave you this book. (Their email address is on the inside back cover.) Then we'll talk about it.

If I can help you be successful … help you harness your demons and decide to pay the price … then I'll feel pretty good about myself.

Some People Wear Me Out!

On the other hand, it wears me out to work with someone who quits. I take it personally. I wonder, "What can I do so this doesn't happen?"

The answer I get? "Make SURE they have a "WHY" ... and make sure it's a 99.9 percenter!"

What motivates you to get up off the couch? What gets you to turn the TV off? What would motivate you to call someone who has asked for information on your business?

So my question is, "How motivated are you?"

Mentoring others gives my life worth and meaning. It drives me. For my personal "WHY", I need YOU to know how motivated you are to do whatever it takes to be successful.

First step is to write down your "WHY." And if you won't pay THAT small price, I want to know now, so I can spend my time with someone who will.

Is Your Biscuit Cooked?

Look. I don't want to yell. **BUT YOU NEED TO PAY ATTENTION HERE!!!**

Write the 3 biggest reasons you MUST be successful. This isn't some namby-pamby, theety-weety dilettante, Barbie doll exercise. This is real life. If you can't do it immediately, then sit there with that blank paper in front of you until you can.

Write your 3 reasons and email them to the email address on the inside back cover of this book

I'll be frank. If you don't do this, then your biscuit isn't cooked! You'll quit so fast, it'll make your head spin.

No "WHY"? No hope!

Ninety percent of the people who start a business will never write down their reasons. So if you do, it's a very, very, very good indicator.

So write your reasons. And make them GOOD!

Only you know if they're good enough for you. So write three, then think some more. Flesh them out. Make them bigger.

Work on them until you say, "Holy mackerel!! THIS is it!"

THEN you're really in business!

#3
A BIG
Research
Surprise

Opportunity Wears A Fake Nose & Mustache

I read a great book back about 1980. Don't remember the title, but it was about luck. Why are people lucky? How does luck happen? Can a cause be pinpointed? What makes lucky people different from unlucky people?

Rabbit's Foot, Anyone?

The author talked to a lot of people, those who considered themselves lucky and those who didn't. He'd find out what had happened in their lives, and he chronicled their incidents of luck.

And then he looked at differences & similarities of the people he'd interviewed, and he came to a conclusion.

His conclusion was a revelation to me. Luck is NOT random.

It's the result of what he called the spider web effect.

People who build webs tend to be lucky. People who don't build webs tend not to be lucky.

In other words … the more contacts you make in life … the more relationships you build … the fewer bridges you burn … the greater the universe of people who have strong positive feeling for you … the more people you reach out to help … the more likely you are to be lucky.

This was fascinating. The biggest conclusion for me was *YOU are in control of your own luck!*

How To Catch Flies

Isn't that amazing? To be lucky, just put out thin lines and thick lines … to people here, there and everywhere.

Doesn't this make perfect sense? The more contacts you have, the more likely you'll be in the right place at the right time. In other words, when one of your contacts runs into a huge opportunity that would be perfect for you, chances are good they'll call YOU.

But if you never make that contact, you'll never hear about the opportunity.

And if you don't make spider webbing a systematic lifetime habit, chances are you'll be one of those people who suffers a lifetime of bad luck.

So build your web continuously, and you greatly increase your chance of being in the path when good things happen.

There's an old saying, "The harder I work, the luckier I get." It's true. Especially if you work at building relationships.

Linda & I have been involved in MLM since 1978, full-time since 1991. We've made lifelong friends, and we've built a good income.

Along the way, we've seen enormous change in the MLM industry.

Give Your Prospects a Puppy

But people haven't changed even the least little bit.

They still want love. They want passion in their personal lives and their professional lives. They want self-satisfaction & health, security & achievement, freedom & trust, fun & financial independence.

People have wanted these same things for a thousand years, and they'll still want them a thousand years from now.

The mistakes I see people make in this business astonish me … the wrong directions they take and the worthless busywork they do.

If you want happiness and fortune & fulfillment in your life, if you want a lifetime of luck, you need to create relationships with people. To do that, you need to study people and understand them. If you will only do that, the opportunities you'll be presented with are endless.

And yet I see so many who want those things … but they study the mold scraped from under the rock by the monk in the white lab coat at midnight on the 7th night after the full moon.

Hey! You definitely need a remarkable product in this business.

But your product is NOT the magic.

The magic is YOU.

The Man Who Stared Down IBM

And I have to tell you, I'm concerned for your future. Consider this carefully:

• Big companies eat small companies. High-paying US jobs go to India. Technologies change overnight. Products come and go. Whole industries fade into history.

• The Soviet Union – one of the world's two superpowers just a few years ago – has disappeared completely.

• Not long ago, IBM was "Big Blue", the ultimate American forward-thinking corporation, hundreds of thousands of employees, invincible. Today, one guy – Michael Dell – sells more personal computers than IBM.

• Companies cut their benefits and your work-hours. HMOs change their terms of delivery. Social Security & Medicare are under enormous stress as the Baby Boomers begin to hit retirement age. Interest groups demand that government DO SOMETHING!

How predictable is YOUR future?

What if you suddenly found yourself with no job, no income, a ton of bills, a family you couldn't feed, the pressure mounting and your hope dwindling?

How would you and your family stand up to that?

Don't say it can't happen. It's happened to countless others over the last 20 years.

And if it did happen, you know what Murphy's Law says?

"Nothing is ever so bad it can't get worse!"

Your Best, Cheapest Solution

In my opinion, your best, least expensive, most-likely-to-work solution is to study people. Study people, and use what you learn to BUILD YOUR SPIDERWEB NOW!!

Obviously, there is no guarantee against catastrophe. But your best protection is to create a huge network of people who you have helped and who feel a kinship & loyalty to you.

We can help you do that. Creating our own giant spiderweb has given Linda & me everything we want in life.

I've written this e-book because we love the network marketing industry, and we want to give back.

Learn what to do. Then build it once, build it right, cherish it and care for it, and it will last and sustain you throughout your lifetime.

The Bad News

It's ironic.

- **Words assault us from every direction, all day long.**

But people talk with each other less than ever.

- **We can name every character on "Friends."**

But we can't name the family who lives 2 doors down.

- **People demand, "What's in it for ME?"**

Then they get all cynical about human nature when nobody stops to help them fix a flat.

- **Big newspapers & TV networks publicly swear by "truth".**

But the truth is, winning a Pulitzer Prize justifies any lie.

- **Big corporations spend a ton on integrated planning and coordination.**

But many would join a cult before they'd spend a nickel on human nature.

- **Direct Marketing gurus call network marketing a rip-off.**

And yet, if you were a fly on the wall when those boys get together, you'd hear them joke with each other about what idiots their own buyers are, and how easy it is to shear those sheep.

If you want to shear sheep, you're in the wrong place.

If you want the "sit back, do nothing, get rich, we'll do all the work for you" plan, I'm not your guy.

The Good News

The good news is all the bad news opens a huge opportunity for you.

Now ... you must TRULY desire to help others.

You can't fake it. You either have it or you don't. People know. Truly caring about others breaks down barriers. As Zig Ziglar said, "You can have everything in life you want, if you help enough other people get what they want."

Trust is the emotion of network marketing. You have to earn it. It comes from consistently doing what's best for your people.

So first, you need people. You must get very good at building personal relationships.

We can help. This book is a great place to start learning.

"Heart" Decisions vs. "Head" Decisions

"Heart" decisions run deeper & last longer than "head" decisions. Direct marketing relationships based on money & product disappear when a competitor upgrades product or lowers price.

But network marketing habits based on higher motivations & emotional connections are hard to break.

If you want to inspire people to learn, grow, develop, succeed, and be all they can be, we can help.

In the end, you must have or develop your own skills & knowledge. And no matter what the future may bring for your company, so long as you gain relationship skills & knowledge, your income is more secure.

If you've started to build your web, and you've treated people right … then if something unexpected happens to ruin a business, your people will follow you to a new one.

THAT is security.

#4
Get "Down 'n Dirty" In MLM

Network Marketing Is NOT What They Tell You

Direct marketing is a numbers game.

Network marketing (MLM) is a relationship game.

Where Network Marketers go wrong is, many are Direct Marketing "wannabes". They're easy to spot by their favorite phrase: "MLM is just a numbers game."

Maybe dazzled by the loot, they shortcut the relationship part of the process.

But the relationship IS the process.
It IS network marketing.

Network marketing is NOT just a numbers game. People are people, not numbers. They have goals, dreams and desires. They are mothers, fathers, sisters, brothers, aunts, uncles, nieces, nephews, grandmothers, and grandfathers to people who love them.

The "numbers game" garbage teaches people to become a recruiter, and not a sponsor. Recruit, recruit, recruit, numbers, numbers, numbers.

The Knife In The Heart

A recruiter never knows their personally sponsored people's "WHY." Or their dreams, goals, or spouse's or children's names. It's only about numbers.

**Products come & go. Companies come & go.
Your spiderweb, if you build it right,
if you treat it right, will last forever.**

If you treat it like just another income source, Direct-Marketing-style, you're trading long-term stability for short-term profit.

I absolutely will not close somebody. This drives the DM guys nuts.

But in network marketing, that's the knife in the heart, to close somebody.

Why?

Because if you had to close them to sign up, then every month you have to call them back to close them to get them to do any work.

They've got to sell themselves. When they see the validity, the strength, the power of what you offer with your coaching, your mentoring, your opportunity, products, service, system, your back office, your front office, your 3-way calling, and so forth, they will sell themselves.

There are a thousand ways to build a network marketing business.

But there is only ONE way to build your spider web for life-long success. And that is to build relationships. To do that, you need to become a mentor with a servant's heart. When you do, people ask you to PLEASE sponsor them into your business.

Look. There's nothing wrong with Direct Marketing. But it is what it is.

Let's talk about Direct Marketing for a minute, and why it appeals to so many.

Have Some ... uh ... WD-40 On That Steak?

Direct marketers sell products directly to the consumer. They are telemarketers, mail-order people, face-to-face salespeople, internet marketers ... and the people who own the companies who perform all these functions.

Direct marketers measure their productivity in numbers. They want bigger, faster, higher, and longer. Buy, or get out of the way. "NEXT!"

To Direct Marketers, "relationship-marketing" has a bottom-line VALUE – the re-orders are better. They search for & discuss with each other the best ways to automate relationship-building.

Automatic relationships!!?

Hey! Have you ever seen a "novelty" T-bone steak? Looks 100% real, but it's plastic.

If "novelty" relationships appeal to you, Network Marketing is not for you.

Speaking of "novelty" relationships ...

Two Ways To Stop Your NEXT Spouse From Demanding a Pre-Nup

The first way is probably the easiest: Don't start a home business. But if you have a good relationship, a successful home business can take you to the next level, with much more family time, and the income to do what you want.

I've seen that many times in MLM, and it's certainly worked that way for Linda & me.

But I've seen other cases where success was the "last straw" in a weak marriage. One spouse or the other saw MLM success as the opportunity to find someone else.

Unfortunately ... quite frequently ... their business then collapses. Life demands its paybacks.

The second way to avoid a pre-nup with your next spouse is sign up with a Direct Marketer. When a direct marketer goes MLM, their motto is, "Recruit, recruit, recruit, sell, sell, sell." And they'll sell you a ton of tapes, advertising, leads, websites and other tools to "help" you recruit people & sell products.

You'll max out your credit cards and empty the checking account.

Later, when your divorce is final, you won't have any assets to worry about anymore ... if you ever find someone else crazy enough to marry you.

What you need is relationship-training. That's non-existent with the DM guys.

Network marketing is a relationship game.

MLM is a relationship business. It's not a sales business. It is not direct marketing. It's you and me working together to create an effect much greater than the sum of the parts.

For instance …

1978 – The Word Picture That Turned My Life Upside Down

In the early 1970s, I learned carpentry and had my own construction business, building homes. One evening in 1978, a gentleman came to our home and said something that really got my attention.

He asked me, "Michael, what if I could show you a way to work for a little bit less money building these homes ... but then those houses would pay you the rest of your life, an ongoing income? Even if you quit and never built any more houses, those checks would keep coming in."

I said, "Man, that's amazing. That's exciting. How is that possible?"

And he said, "Well, there's an opportunity that creates residual income like that. You work hard today, and create a 'mailbox' income, that comes in even if you quit doing it."

That was THE first time I'd ever heard of network marketing. I'd spent 7 years busting my back, working, slaving and building in my carpentry business. The thought of getting paid in the future for work I do now really caught my attention.

The REAL Truth About Network Marketing

And he said, "The fact is, YOU have done network marketing, word-of-mouth advertising, every day, since about age 5. You told your mom & dad what sneakers you wanted, your favorite cereal, shirts, baseball gloves, books, movies, restaurants, all kinds of things. You've been promoting since about age 5. But you've never gotten paid for it.

"With my company, you get to pick up that check."

So Linda & I looked at what they were doing. We joined that opportunity. And that company eventually was bought out by another company that's still in existence today.

And we actually still get checks today from that business we did 25 years ago! Isn't that incredible?

Now THAT is a spider web!

If you want to create that type of situation, the place you start is with relationship-building. I'll help you. A total recluse, who REALLY wanted to, could actually learn to get good at Network Marketing.

How?

Learn about people. Study people. Build your spider web. Build it right. Build it once. Mentor your contacts to do the same. If you care for it, it will last forever, no matter what opportunities may come & go.

But you must remember this:

The Boy Scout's Oath

Your first commitment MUST be to your people, NOT to personal profit.

For most Direct Marketers, the #1 commitment is personal profit. That's neither right nor wrong, it's just Direct Marketing. The bad effect is that many of them will sell anything and everything, without ever trying it themselves (as many online affiliate marketers do, for instance).

When network marketers do that, trust & loyalty disappear. Your web disintegrates. You have no hope.

My Mentor – The Most Brilliant Marketer I Know …

… Is Tom "Big Al" Schreiter. And let me tell you why.

He travels the world doing his little 2 or 3-hour seminars. He charges maybe $5 to cover the cost of the room. Sometimes it's free.

Why does he do this?

Because he also owns a network marketing company. And when he goes to Tampa, Florida, he usually has 2 or 3 leaders in his company who he meets there. He takes them to dinner. He buys them lunch. He builds a relationship with them. He shakes their hand.

You will never ever ever ever ever EVER be able to get money out of your pocket and pay for anything when you're around Tom Schreiter. He's buying you lunch, he's buying you dinner. If 20 people go, he's buying for everybody.

This has NEVER been a numbers game to Tom Schreiter. He builds these relationships because he knows a little secret about network marketing.

Sometime in the history of your company, they'll put the labels on the products crooked. They'll be back-ordered on something, because people run the business. There are imperfections. He knows that.

So he builds a relationship with his people so that when the labels are crooked, or the bonus check is late, or they back-ordered the product ... he knows that you won't quit. You won't quit, because you have that relationship with him. He makes sure of that personally, one on one.

We do it with our coaching calls. The secret of network marketing is retention, retention, retention, retention.

Keep Your People Or DIE!

To have a chance to build relationships and get that retention, you must:

1. Choose a company with consumable products that make a real difference in the lives of your people and those they love. **Network marketing is a relationship business, and it's also a TESTIMONIAL business.** For your people to be successful with word-of-mouth advertising, they need a strong testimonial for the products they like.

2. Offer great value to the end user (and the value YOU offer includes much more than just your products), which allows you to build a very attractive income.

3. Get to know your people. Learn what they really want. Help them formulate their "WHY". Do everything you can to make them feel so valued & cared for that they'll be forever loyal. Give them the personal attention, respect & admiration they deserve.

If your people see you as a DM genius, you're lost in space.

If they see you as a special, trusted friend
& confidante, you're right on track.

Of course, there ARE DMers who do it right:

Joyce Clyde Hall rose from poverty to create & build Hallmark Cards. In the early 1950s, he started the Hallmark Hall of Fame, TV's longest-running – and BEST – dramatic series. The shows are consistently great.

Even the commercials – now branded in our everyday language as "Hallmark Moments" – touch your heart.

Hallmark proves that focusing on quality, loyalty and building relationships are not just the right thing to do … it's profitable.

MLM Is a Moving Parade

People join. People quit. Some never even start – they peak when they sign the application.

You want coachable people with a strong desire & work ethic. They'll build your business. You'll recognize them, because they'll raise their hands and tell you who they are. They will send you their "WHY." You then mentor them to productivity, and they become part of your spider web.

Now … you can't treat people like numbers. But the more people you talk with, the better chance you'll run into the one who ALREADY has a web of thousands and brings a ton of monthly income for you. That happens when you work this business.

Did you know that most Americans at
age 65 have a minus net worth?
You and I can't change that.

DM will NEVER help them.

The ONLY Person To Spend Your Time On

But you & I can sure help a few of them …the ones who tell us they want our help. It's not up to you to chase them down. **You're looking for someone who's looking for you.**

When you find them, mentor them, and train them to build their own web. Those are the people who return the trust and loyalty that make this such a wonderful business.

Do The ONLY Thing That Matters!

10 Mistakes Everybody Makes Selling Hamburgers

Let's say you & I are each opening fast-food restaurants. And we make a side bet about who can sell the most hamburgers.

What advantages would you most want to help you win our bet?

You want Grade A Black Angus beef?

Sesame seed buns?

You want a tasty veggie burger for the non meat-eaters?

The best, crispiest fries?

Ambience? An atmosphere where people love to come?

Or maybe uncomfortable chairs ... so they eat and get out in a hurry?

A playground for the kids?

Lowest price? You want THAT, too?

You are one tough cookie. That is for sure.

But OK. Done, done, done, done, done, done, and done!

What's that? You say I'm holding back?

You want the best location, too?

Oh. My. God! You're killing me here!

OK, fine. You get the busiest crossroads in town.

Matter of fact, I'll give you ALL OF IT!
Every advantage you want, you've got!

Satisfied?

Good for you.

Myself, I only want ONE advantage. And if you give it to me, when it comes to selling hamburgers, I'll whip the pants off you.

The only advantage I want is ... a MOB OF STARVING PEOPLE!

You've Got a TON of Homework Tonight!

In MLM, I see people all the time who study, study, study, research, research, research ... to find the PERFECT product. Some spend months or even YEARS preparing to actually DO something!

It sounds crazy, I know. But I swear, it's true.

Fact is, there are a TON of products in the MLM world that are 90%-great, or better. And whether you have a 91%-great product or a 96%-great product has ZERO bearing on whether you are successful or not.

So just pick a good product. TODAY!!

Then spend your time studying people ... and learn how to find the people STARVING for what you offer.

What do your distributors & customers want most passionately?

How do their desires drive them to a buying decision?

What gets them in a frenzy when they look for an opportunity? What makes them turn away and look for greener pastures?

Do you REALLY think it's your product or your compensation plan?

MLM is first and foremost a people business.

Period.

It's you and me together creating an effect much greater than just the sum of the parts.

It's profitable because your people use your products. And you also get paid when THEIR people use your products, on down a few levels.

Take a Bus Driver To Lunch

No matter what you learn in this lifetime, nothing will be more emotionally or financially rewarding than learning about people.

It's worth your while to spend time with people you don't know, who do jobs you'd never dream of doing, just to listen to them, find out about them, ask questions.

I'm not talking about recruiting. I'm talking about relating.

Any time you spend now getting to understand other people & how they think, will reward you many times over in the future.

Work Smart – Fail Forward

If you could work for 3 years and build something that pays you $50,000 a month, wouldn't you rather do that than build something that only pays you $5,000 a month?

Linda & I started in 1978, and we just "failed forward." We worked until the wheels got knocked out from under us for one reason or another.

Then we went at it again.

It took time. We failed forward until I finally found a mentor in 1991. I found someone who was successful, who had already done it. I bought every tape, book, etc., that he ever did.

Nail Your Prospect's Passionate Sweet Spot

I learned everything from Tom "Big Al" Schreiter. I plugged in, absorbed it all.

I'd listen completely to his albums while driving. I've made a ton of notes driving down the Interstate.

Never crashed, either.

One question I'd hear over and over was,

"Why Do Some People Succeed, While Others NEVER Do?"

And the answer that kept coming up over and over again was, successful people made the effort to understand what really makes people tick ... what motivates them ... why they make the choices they make.

That is what really led me into the personality studies.

400 years before Jesus Christ, the Greek physician and philosopher Hippocrates wrote about the four basic personality types.

In 1921, Dr. Carl Jung wrote the most detailed book ever on this subject. He called the 4 personality types Feeler, Sensor, Thinker, and Intuitive.

Florence Littauer later named them Phlegmatic, Sanguine, Melancholy, and Choleric.

Since then, many others have written books and recorded audiotapes on the subject, including:

- Michael O'Connor
- Kathryn Briggs
- Dr. Tony Alessandra
- Jim Cathcart
- Tim Lahaye
- Dr. Bernice McCarthy
- Jerry Clark

My personal thanks to all who have contributed to the personality-type knowledge base. Their research & conclusions are the basis for our mentor training.

Color To Success

I know of no other subject that when used correctly can have such a positive impact on your life and your business.

This stuff works.

People fall asleep when you say "phlegmatic, sanguine, melancholy and choleric". But they understand colors. And you can easily learn to color your way to the top.

You can get the full training CD from the source on the inside back cover of this book. Just email them and request the information on how to get the CD.

Following is a brief synopsis of our training:

Yellows

Yellows make up 35% of the population. They are nurses, schoolteachers, UN workers ... the nurturers. They give from the heart. They don't have time for themselves, because they give to everybody.

Yellows have built some of the largest organizations in network marketing ... WHEN they have the belief they can do it.

How To Sponsor A Yellow

To color your way to the top, you need to learn to be a chameleon.

Yellows don't want to be sold. They don't like pushy, aggressive salespeople.

When you talk with a Yellow, become a Yellow. Slow the pace. Contain your excitement. Lower the volume. Yellows see excitement as hype, you trying to sell them. Don't tell a Yellow about making $10,000 a month, because they'll turn right off.

Instead, visit with them. Skip the business. Talk about their family, their kids, their vacation.

Yellows cannot work in stair step breakaway-type compensation plans. They have to be in a plan where you can put people under people and people under people. They're best in any kind of "infinity" plan that pays them to work deep, deep, deep.

They'll never be happy in a unilevel or a stair step breakaway plan where you put 5 people on your front line, until you hit a certain volume amount, then you put another 5 people on your front line, etc.

Success in this plan requires all your time spent on massive first level recruiting. This doesn't work for Yellows.

MLM industry stats show the average network marketer only ever sponsors 2.7 people.

So if your Yellow sponsors 3 people ... if they have to go 5 wide, then they haven't done anything. But at 2 wide, then they can put 1 of their 3 underneath somebody.

And other average people can sponsor 3.

Now you've got some spillover. And then here and there you get a serious business-builder who sponsors 8 or 10 people a month, and you get more spillover. When more people work together, you get more synergy. So THAT compensation plan works great with the Yellows.

Blues

BLUEs "just wanna have fun." They're 15% of the population. They're always in a sales business of some kind. They jump from program to program to program, looking for fun. These are the planet's most creative people.

A Blue sees the big picture instantly. They don't need or want all the details. Blues can eat an elephant, but not at one meal.

How To Sponsor A Blue

They're same as the Yellows as far as the comp plan. In the same comp plan, they can go deep, to create massive spillover and a lot of stuff happening quickly for them. That gets them excited, and they'll stay in the business.

With a Blue, talk excited, get excited. Talk about going scuba diving, sky diving, having fun, fun, fun. That's what they want. "Hey, when you meet me at the airport, I'll be wearing a Hawaiian shirt. You'll know me. I'll have a big, funny hat on." That's what they want to talk about.

They'll talk about vacations & family, but most of all they want to talk about fun things to do.

Greens

Greens are 35% of the population. They're the analytical people. They analyze it to death. They've missed millions of dollars in opportunities because they analyzed it too long.

Greens can take Blue's idea to the next level. They work well in any type of complicated compensation plan. They like to figure out the Super Star Space Commander bonus that's paid out on the 3rd, 9th, & 12th levels, every other full moon.

How To Sponsor A Green

Greens believe they're the smartest people on the planet. With a Green ... in 2-3 minutes, you'll know you have a Green. They want ALL the details.

You are NOT going to sell them. Don't even try. They have to sell themselves. They'll go to the web site, they'll listen to the conference call. Then they'll go to the next website and the next link. If you have 27 links on your website, they'll go to every one. They'll read all the testimonials, all the articles, etc.

Enunciate all your words correctly for a Green. Don't speak too fast. Don't speak too slow. Be upfront. Give them all the information. Answer all their questions. Give them more websites to go to.

If you call in the meantime to answer questions, they'll be abrupt. They see that as you being pushy. Let Greens analyze the information at THEIR pace.

In a week or 2 or 3, they'll call back for more information or ready to start. They've sold themselves; decided this is the perfect business.

Greens want to feed a Blue the elephant in one meal. And that's the way the Green will build the business.

Reds

Reds are 15% of the population. They are money-motivated, money-focused. Don't bother talking to them about your family or your vacation. They don't care.

They know if you get married, you're supposed to have kids. If you have kids, you're supposed to go on vacation. End of story. Don't want to talk about it.

How To Sponsor A Red

They want to talk about the money, the money, the money.

Reds do well in a stair step breakaway compensation plan, because they think network marketing is a sales business. For them, it's sell, sell, sell. In a stair step plan, they can put 5 people on their front line. If only one produces, they never go back and put somebody underneath them. They're just looking for producers, somebody who will build, build, build.

The Red knows that once that first productive person in the first group of 5 hits $50,001 volume, they'll then break away. And the Red's override drops from 15% to 5%, because the other 10% goes to the person who built it.

That's fine for the Red, because they understand their job is to find another Red and keep getting those 5% retentions. For them, it's a sales business.

Reds are the corporate CEOs, the "get-the-job-done" people, the ones everyone in network marketing is looking for.

But it's a fallacy. Reds are just 15% of the population, and they are absolutely not coachable. They have the biggest egos. They order people around. It works in corporate America, but not in network marketing.

When a Red demands that people get on conference calls, he drives his people away.

On the other hand, Reds are well-connected. You want to sponsor Reds because they'll put you in contact with powerful people. They know business owners, governors, leaders, etc.

So target Reds. But don't dare think you're going to coach them or mentor them or tell them what to do, because it's NOT going to happen.

Let them do it themselves. You really have no choice, anyway.

**But network marketing is NOT a sales business.
It's a teaching and mentoring business.**

That's what I learned early from Tom "Big Al" Schreiter.

When you find people massively successful in a stair step breakaway type comp plan, they are the Reds, the salespeople. But with that type plan, retention is very low. If they recruit 100 people in a year, they've got just a handful left by the end of the year.

But with a Yellow, if they get 100 people in the business, they'll teach & mentor. They'll work down deep in the organization and they may have 60 or 70 still active after a year.

Saddam Hussein Meets Dr. Phil

Everyone is a blend of colors, showing different personality traits at different times. Now I've never met Saddam Hussein, but from what I've seen, he seems a pretty "hard sell" guy to me. Very red. And lesser amounts of analytical, fun-loving & caring for people.

Wouldn't you agree?

My guess would be 75% Red, 12% Green, 8% Blue, 5% Yellow.

So what would happen if Saddam met, say … Dr. Phil?

My guess on Dr. Phil is maybe 40% Yellow, 25% Red, 25% Blue, and 10% Green.

THAT meeting might make the News at 11.

What's the point?

Well, as you meet and LISTEN to people, get in the habit of spotting the different colors in their personalities. Use the clues we talked about. Use the "colors" technique every day. Make it second nature. I guarantee you'll be very glad you did.

Opportunity Has VERY Long Legs

Another observation here is that 85% of the population (Blues, Greens & Yellows) either work best or work very well with network marketing compensation plans that pay down deep or to infinity. Reds (15%) are much better with unilevel (unlimited width) plans.

Decide for yourself, but it's always good to have the percentages as much in your favor as possible.

A Concept That Changed My Life

I can't even begin to tell you how different my life is since learning how to spot and work with each of these personalities.

Maybe the biggest change is this: to spot these personalities, you must LISTEN to people! And wonderful things seem to happen when you actually listen.

Everyone is a blend of all these colors. Personally, I'm 40% Blue, 30% Red, 20% Green, & 10% Yellow. But I've learned to be a chameleon to deal with people.

Used to be when I came across a Green (35% of the population, remember?), I saw someone who took forever to make a decision. They'd analyze it to death.

They drove me crazy. So I'd blow them off. I wouldn't even return their phone calls.

But look at this ... I was losing 35% of my prospects! And when a Green joins, they never quit. They're not like the Blues. You can put a Blue in the business tonight, but they'll never do anything. They'll never even activate their business. They'll just join, because they thought it would be fun. But the Blues, again, will put you in contact with a lot of good people.

So the biggest secret for me was learning that network marketing is not a sales business.

It's a teaching & mentoring business.
No wonder the Yellows & the Greens are so good at MLM.
AND they make up 70% of the population!

So let the Yellows & the Greens know that it's not their fault. The cards have been stacked against them in network marketing. And the Reds have been telling everybody the whole time that it's a sales business. Sell, sell, sell.

It has NOTHING to do with selling. It has EVERYTHING to do with teaching, training, coaching, and mentoring people.

YOU: Robo-Bonder!

This technology will connect you with the deepest desires and needs and fears of the people you set out to bond with. It won't be long before you actually know these people better than they know themselves.

The sad fact is that most people are too self-absorbed to ever actually use this training. It is worth an absolute FORTUNE to those who do.

When you listen to people and truly understand their personality, you can help inspire them to greatness. The rewards for you are WAY more than just financial.

On the other hand, if all that matters to you is YOU, you really don't have a prayer in this business.

For us, learning these secrets was a life-changer.

If you'd like to learn complete details about recognizing and dealing with each of these personality types, and if you'd like to hear EXACTLY what we say on the phone to each type, get a copy of our CD course, **"Color To Success"**.

Just send an email to the source on the inside back cover of this book requesting info on how to get the "Colors" CD, and they'll email you the details.

Three Very Revealing Quizzes For You:
Do You Think Like A Prospect?

Some things just cannot possibly be said any better. This first article is one of them. It's a piece I'm borrowing from Ed Thorpe who writes "The Home Grown Biz Advocate Ezine". You can visit Ed on the web at http://www.lazydudepublishing.com.
His article really sets up our main quiz today. Here it is:

The Charles Schultz Lesson
By Edward Thorpe

If you're like me, you've probably asked yourself "Hm, what kinda person am I? Am I a good, honest, caring person?" etc.

What I'm getting at . . .

We all have some ideas about who we are and what we stand for, wouldn't you agree? Because you're here and you don't yet know me, you deserve to know what kinda guy I am.

Actually, I couldn't tell you the things important to me, any better than Charles Schultz, the creator of the much-loved 'Peanuts' cartoon series, did.

The following was written by the late Charles Schultz and is a darn near perfect description of how I view life in general.

(You don't actually have to take the quiz below. Just read it straight through. You'll get the point.)

"The Charles Schultz Philosophy!"

1. Name the five wealthiest people in the world.
2. Name the last five Heisman trophy winners.
3. Name the last five winners of the Miss America contest.
4. Name any ten people who have won the Nobel or Pulitzer prize.
5. Name the last half dozen Academy Award winners for best actor.
6. Name the last decade's World Series winners.

"How did you do?"

The point is, none of us remember the headliners of yesterday.

These are no second-rate achievers. They are the best in their fields. But the applause dies. Awards tarnish.

Achievements are forgotten. Accolades and certificates are buried with their owners.

Anatomy of a Prospect's Mind

Here's another quiz. See how you do on this one:

1. List a few teachers who aided your journey through school.
2. Name three friends who have helped you through a difficult time.
3. Name five people who have taught you something worthwhile.
4. Think of a few people who have made you feel appreciated and special.
5. Think of five people you enjoy spending time with.
6. Name half a dozen heroes whose stories have inspired you.

"Easier?"

The big lesson:

The people who make a difference in your life are not the ones with the most credentials, the most money, or the most awards.

They are the ones that care.

Pass this on to those people who have made a difference in your life. And don't worry about the world coming to an end today. It's already tomorrow in Australia.

Written by "Peanuts" Creator, Charles Schultz...The SAME man who couldn't get a cartoonist job at The Disney Corporation...

Some 'boss' at Disney told Charles he lacked talent and was not creative.

Key Point: Don't let others 'label' you. Mr. Schultz didn't. Follow his lead. Follow your heart. Live your life for "You".

Again, thanks to Ed Thorpe, publisher of ""The Home Grown Biz Advocate Ezine," (http://www.lazydudepublishing.com) for this article.

Now it's time for

My Quiz For You

My mentor, Tom "Big Al" Schreiter, has traveled the world promoting his MLM business. He's discovered what prospects consider most important in deciding on a company.

Rate these items yourself, from 1 to 10, most important to least important.

I strongly encourage you to REALLY do this exercise. It will take maybe 5 minutes. Then I'll give you the REAL answers from prospects around the world.

And if you discover THEIR thinking is radically different from YOUR thinking ... well, that could explain a lot!

One more thing: #1 in this poll won by a LANDSLIDE. It wasn't even close. So it should be real easy for YOU to get #1 right.

Right?

OK. Let's do it!

Get your pen. Here's the list:

- Company literature shown
- Marketing plan and potential earnings
- Training provided
- Who gave the presentation
- Product line
- Company management experience
- Up-line support
- Company image
- Sales kit provided
- Being first in your area

Now just list those down from 1 to 10, most important to least important, from the prospect's point of view.

Do it now.

The key question is, "Are you thinking like a prospect?

NO, NO, NO!

No peeking until you've numbered your list!

OK. #1, and it won by a landslide is:

1. Who Gave the Presentation?

Is that a surprise? It's about YOU. People join people, they don't join companies. So the most important item to prospects by a landslide is "who gave the presentation?"

Again, that's from a prospect standpoint. Maybe to us it's more important to know the company name, how long it's been in business, who's the founder, and so forth.

But the prospect wants to know exactly who gave the presentation. This is a people business. When you care about people, they relate to that.

2. Upline Support

Back to YOU again, the 2nd most important factor, again by a landslide. Prospects need to know if YOU will be of any help to them. And will the up-line be any help?

So number one is, people join people ... but #2 is pretty much the same. They want to know if they can do it. And we're definitely not going to join somebody we don't like, because then we'd have to work with them.

3. Training Provided

Look at this! They aren't even wondering about money yet, we haven't talked about a company, we're still talking about YOU. #3 is about you again. Do you have a conference call we can plug into? Do you have some systems in place to help us be successful? Do you have training? Does the company do training? Are you a good sponsor? Will you help me?

A LOT of people aren't sure they can do this. Maybe it's their first exposure to network marketing. But if they know they'll be trained by someone who's good, that raises their belief level.

One thing I do with my people, when I work with someone or when I sponsor someone I tell them please, please, listen to this specific tape. Or read this book. And I tell them please do not talk to anybody.

I don't want you to go try to sell your friends & family. Let me work with you, help you get educated in this business. We'll work together to get you successful.

So it's critical that you help that person and give them the training they need.

I know some new people get just the opposite. You join and the first thing you hear is, "OK. Let's go hammer the phones. Make your list today. We'll start calling tomorrow at 5:00PM when you get off work."

I'm saying, "Back up! Don't burn that bridge."

If I just joined your business and had no idea what I was talking about, I'd probably say the wrong thing. I'd get excited and leave things out. You're excited that you joined, but let's say the right thing, not burn that warm market.

4. Marketing Plan and Potential Earnings

So we're almost halfway through the list. And NOW the prospect is finally wondering, "Can I make some money?" It's not really about can they make some money. It's more, can YOU train me? Can YOU help me make money?

And how much money isn't the issue. It's just, "Can I do this and make some money?"

So 1, 2, & 3 were about you. Then we finally get to money. They want to know a little about the compensation plan. Don't go into great detail, because they probably won't understand much of it, anyway.

5. Product Line

We finally get to products. Are you paying close attention? Because if you've got a prospect, and you try to tell them the secret ingredients, how the product works or how your long distance service switches work, how deep the cables are buried or whatever your product or service is ...

... then you're going at this bass ackwards!

People don't care about that stuff. They just want to know, What's the product? Can I use it? Don't waste your time teaching them how many grams of sodium it has. Keep it simple.

Let's recap.

First, they need to like the person who did the presentation. So you need to learn a bit about them and identify with them.

Next, they want to make sure they can do it. They want to believe.

Third, they want to make sure you and the people you work with can train them.

Then comes money.

Then comes product line.

Is that how you had the first 5 on YOUR list? Do you follow this order of importance when you talk to people?

What you should remember:

People join people. They don't join companies.

6. Being First In the Area

Have you noticed we haven't even talked about the company yet, but we're being first in the area? People don't want to blaze a trail, but they do want to see there's a large potential to have some growth there.

7. Company Literature Shown

There are a LOT of networkers who focus on the literature. But this isn't a reading business. It's a relationship business. If you don't believe that, take a look at the top 3 on this list again.

If you're relying on a sales brochure to sell someone or an audiotape or a videotape, you'd better think again. It's back to you.

If I have a real nice 3D presentation, holograms, smoke and lights, that's great. But if I don't connect with people on a personal level, nothing else matters.

8. Company Image

Maybe you show a video featuring a 20,000 square foot office & warehouse, on three acres in an exclusive suburb, all the bells & whistles.

Big whoop. That's #8 on their list, barely on the radar. Why bother?

They just need to know the company is there, it's legitimate, not hiding behind some post office box or working out of a storage unit. It'll send them a check. That's basically all they care about at this point.

So we're almost to the end of what's important to prospects. But I've been to a lot of presentations, and "Company Image" tends to be the FIRST thing shown & mentioned.

"Hi. My company name is Blah-Blah. They're great. I'm now going to waste 20 minutes of your valuable time & tell you all about them."

A lot of presentations that are done backwards, from a prospect's angle ... which is the ONLY angle that matters.

9. Is The Sales Kit Provided?

Now the prospect wants to know that you do have a good video, you do have good literature, you've got tools and services they can use to build their business.

So YOU are still the most important thing and the sales kit is almost the least important thing!

But how many presentations have you seen where first they talk about the company, then they show the sales kit?

Prospects don't care. They need to know if you can help them, if the upline can help them. Can they make some money? Can you help them be successful?

Which brings us to our final item ...

10. Company Management Experience

LEAST important to the prospect is that the president is a family man, and he's got four or five families to prove it.

It does not matter to the prospect.

So this whole process is way simpler than most people think:

1. Make sure they like you.

2. Make sure they believe they can do it.

If you don't do those two, nothing else matters.

Think about all this for a second.

You're talking to a prospect. You start off with the company management experience, which is the least important thing to them.

Now your prospect is leaning back, eyes are glazed over, zoned-out, nodding off.

They've heard it all before, and they just don't care.

But what if you start with the most important thing first - YOU!

Tell them a story about your experience in the business (or your upline's experience, if you're new). Tell them how you work with people, and exactly what you'll do to help them be successful.

THAT is what prospects want.

OK. It's time to score your quiz.

Take the difference between what you had and the correct answer. (E.g., if you had #10 Company Management experience ranked #1, you'd have a difference of 9.

Do that with every item. Add them up. Now you'll see how YOU are thinking, compared to how the prospect is thinking.

When I took this test myself, I scored a twelve. What that taught me was, I was thinking more like the prospect. But remember, I've been at this since 1978.

A friend of mine with an insurance background took this test. He scored a very high number. He was thinking like the company owner, not like a prospect.

To him, when you sell life insurance, you tell them the company is a hundred years old they're A+ rated. You give them all your flyers and brochures. It's all company, company, company. The least important thing was him.

So when he turned around those two things he had number 1 as number 10 and number 10 as number 1. When he turned those around in his mind his score was almost the same as mine.

I'll bet there are a ton of networkers who look at this backwards.

It doesn't matter if you're a well-trained networker or completely new. You have to think like a prospect. What you know doesn't matter. It's what your prospect thinks that matters.

A lot of people have quit in this industry. You do a presentation and the prospect says, "Well, you know what? I already tried this and it doesn't work."

Or maybe one of your people sponsors someone new. And the first person they go to says, "You know what? I tried one of those things, they really don't work."

Why do you think most people fail in network marketing? They quit because something happened. Why do you think most people fail?

Of course, some people are just quitters. They quit school, they quit marriages, they quit jobs, they just quit because that's what they do.

Talk Their Talk, And Walk Their Walk

But what I've learned in network marketing is the biggest reason people fail is, they fail to get educated about people.

If you were a ditch digger, a doctor, a lawyer, a carpenter, or a plumber, you'd have to get educated. Network marketing is no different.

You need to read books. Listen to audiotapes. Most important, find a mentor.

When a young person decides to become a doctor, they go to school for 8 years first. They create ZERO income over those 8 years. They just study and go to school.

Then they get out with a chance to make an income.

In network marketing, you can get educated and build your business at the same time. After 8 years of getting educated and building your business you can be making 10 times the money that a doctor will make.

So you have to get yourself educated first. Learn what makes people tick. You've been doing network marketing since age 5, recommending products since age 5. You have a TON of experience doing this!

You've just never picked up the check before.

So you're doing it since age 5. Nobody's every arrested you for recommending and promoting your favorite cereal or restaurant or movie. So it must be legal.

You have experience. You don't need any special degree to get started and be successful.

I'd bet you will NEVER quit recommending or promoting things to other people.

You may just as well pick up the check.

When you get your people to understand that, they will never quit.

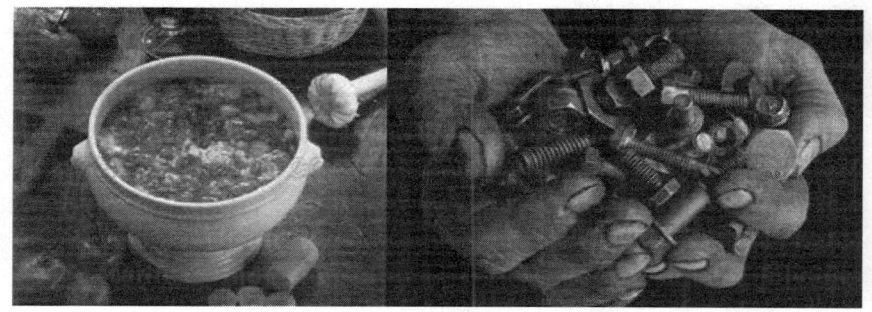

#7
Your MLM Business
From Soup To Nuts

For MLM veterans, the next 2 pages will be review. For newcomers, you'll get up to speed.

Why do people want a home business?

Why do so many choose MLM, or network marketing?

And EXACTLY what tools do you need to be successful in this business?

Surveys show that as many as 85% of Americans would LOVE to earn money from home.

The 4 reasons most don't go for it?

1. High $$ investment
2. Too much time required
3. High risk
4. They don't have a clue how to get started.

If You Want To Be A Winner,
Raise Your Hand

A home business offers the following:

1. No Boss. Plan your own workday. Monitor yourself. Set priorities. Set it up so it's fun for YOU.

2. No income ceiling.

3. Self-satisfaction. YOU create the business. YOU get credit.

4. Work with people you like. No difficult co-workers. No office politics.

5. Flexibility. Work the hours you want to fit in with your life & family. If your best working hours are 2 am to 5 am, you're free to do that.

6. No commuting. Save time & money.

7. No office expense = quicker profit.

8. Security. No layoffs. No downsizing.

9. Tax deductions: home office, car expense, medical insurance, phone, entertainment, travel, education, etc.

10. Better retirement plan: SEP IRAs & Keoghs let you deduct a higher percent of business profit than your 401K.

Additional benefits of an *MLM* opportunity:

1. Low start-up cost: You can probably get everything you need to start, including leads to follow up with, for less than $300. Most businesses take thousands of dollars in start-up capital.

2. No expensive training. In fact, I'll train you and ALL your people to succeed in this business, 5 nights a week on the phone at 8 pm Eastern time, for FREE!

3. No administration hassles. You're self-employed, but you're a rep for an established company which handles all the product selection, research & development, shipping, warehousing, etc.

4. Keep your regular job until your "part-time" income is high enough to replace it.

5. No expensive tools necessary. You need a phone. A computer is helpful. But your most critical tool is people skills, and we will teach you those FREE!

And Finally, The 8th Wonder of the World:

6. Residual Income. You profit from the product purchases & sales of everyone in your group.

Nothing is more important to your financial future than the "residual income" concept. Let's dig into it a bit.

To qualify for a paycheck, you must purchase X amount of product each month. When you sponsor someone, you get monthly commissions on THEIR product purchases, for as long as they re-order. To increase your monthly income, just add NEW distributors to your organization.

You also profit on your ENTIRE group's purchases. Once you've built a big group, most of your income comes from the work of others. (Which beats the heck out of an hourly wage and ZERO income when you don't work!)

An MLM home based business pays into the future for work you did in the past. As you help your people build their own organizations, YOUR income grows.

Which means there's a HUGE incentive to your sponsor to help YOU succeed, since they get a percentage of the sales in your group.

So to be successful fastest, align yourself with a group that provides a turnkey plan for the crucial elements of building your business:

1. Lead Generation
2. Prospect follow-up
3. Sponsoring
4. Training your reps to do exactly the same thing.

Blues Just Want To Have Fun!

I'm a big believer in fun. (Told you before I'm 40% BLUE.)

In fact, if it's NOT fun, you won't catch me within 20 miles of it.

Writing a book should be fun. READING one should definitely be fun.

And building a business for life should be CONSTANT FUN! Mine has been.

Yours should be, too.

Some VERY Bad Un-Fun

Failing at building a business. THAT is very bad un-fun.

The way I see a lot of people fail is, especially in the internet age, they get started and then they go WAY off in some other direction, not even realizing they're getting farther and farther from their goal. (Solutions for this in Chapter 10.)

Because of the internet, it is simpler than ever to set up a step-by-step system to do the lead generation, follow-up, sponsoring & training functions.

But the internet bulges with clutter and infinite choices. So the task of identifying, coordinating, and implementing the components necessary for success is often hopelessly confusing, way beyond the abilities of mortal man (or woman).

Ironic, isn't it?

The Human Winning Machine

If YOU were your prospect, what would YOU want?

I know what I'd want.

1. When you talked with me, I'd want you to LISTEN first and foremost, to find out what I really want. I'd need to feel you and I were simpatico.

This is where you must kick butt. Start your relationship-building immediately. TELL me what you're doing and WHY you're doing it, and let me know that part of your system is to help me build those key relationships.

I want to believe you consider MY success crucial to your life.

Michael Jordan was the greatest basketball player ever. A big part of that was, he just plain WANTED to win more than the other guys.

You ever watch Jordan the last few minutes of a close game – ANY close game? He CHANGED!! He'd psyche himself into a zone where he could virtually do no wrong. He had total disdain for whomever he was playing.

He didn't just want to beat them. He wanted to EMBARRASS them!

He'd focus on his skills and become a human winning machine.

YOU need the same focus when you talk to your prospect. The ONLY thing that matters is what your prospect thinks, wants, wishes for, desires and needs.

If I'm your prospect, YOUR entire universe better revolve around me when we talk. What YOU want doesn't even exist, as far as I'm concerned. And it shouldn't exist for you, either … not when you're talking to me.

THEN you and I will have an identical viewpoint!

2. I would want you to make a very clear, short, compelling case – based on what I've told you – as to why YOUR opportunity is better for me than all the competition.

I'd expect you to be able to answer every marketing question I have.

Don't tap dance around what you don't know. Know your company resources well enough to get me to the exact right source (hotlines, web pages, brochures, etc.) to answer any questions you can't answer.

3. I would want a simple marketing system that's inviting, informative, non-threatening, educational, & fun.

The more complex it is, the less chance I'll be able to execute. You are in a cutthroat contest for my time and attention. One of your key weapons in this battle is simplicity. Making the complex clear is hard work. Few people do it well.

If you can give me all the information I need, clear & organized so I can make a quick choice, your chances skyrocket.

Plus – it helps YOU work smarter.

A System That Works

Again ... you need to do lead generation, prospect follow-up, sponsoring and training. If you can do them all with one system, so much the better. If your company or group does not provide systems to accomplish these actions, you will absolutely have to set them up yourself. It's a lot easier to go someplace where they're already established.

> **You can have a lead generation system that brings ONLY the most qualified people into your group. Then I'll train them FREE, 5 nights a week, to build relationships and become Top Sponsors who will build YOU a lifetime residual income!**

How does this work?

1. Get visitors to your website (see step 2 for your website).

There are a ton of ways to get visitors to your site. If you can't spend money on traffic generation, that's OK. Many effective traffic generation methods are free.

And even if you can afford to buy all the traffic you'll ever need, many of your reps won't be able to. So you are best to start NOW learning how to generate traffic at zero or very low cost. We offer free tutorials on dozens of free or low-cost online traffic generation techniques and websites, giving you exact steps to get started. Just email your source listed on the inside back cover of this book, and they will send you the information.

2. Look at the *"Success In 10 Steps"* website listed on the inside back cover of this book.

This is our opt-in page where people can order the *"Success In 10 Steps"* e-book. The page is designed to appeal to people who want to make money from home, and who are readers. In my experience, Leaders are Readers.

Your website has only one objective: capture contact information. So signing up is the ONLY option a person has when they get to your site.

A lead that is a reader is far more likely to have long-term success than most other leads you get.

For just a few dollars a month, you can have your own **Success In 10 Steps** website to drive traffic to. The resulting leads will go right to you.

3. What To Do With Your Leads

I do a live, generic MLM training call 5 nights a week.

No company is EVER mentioned on these calls.
No products are EVER discussed.

You can bring your lead phone numbers to that call, and you and I will call them together. You'll hear exactly what to say. We'll establish that they're definitely looking for a good way to make extra money from home. Then we'll set a time for you to call them back to talk more in depth about YOUR opportunity.

You'll get to listen in while I work with other callers, talking to their leads, too.

4. How to Sponsor Them Into Your Opportunity

Refer back to Chapter 5. Above all else, to be successful in sponsoring people, you need to understand people. You need to listen to them. You need our Colors Training. I can't stress how critical this is to your success. To get the Colors Training CD, just email or call your contact listed on the inside back cover of this book, and they will tell you how to get the CD.

And you will be able to make an offer to your people that's very difficult to refuse – namely, OUR offer:

> **You can have a lead generation system that brings ONLY the most qualified people into your group. Then I'll train them FREE, 5 nights a week, to build relationships and become Top Sponsors who will build YOU a lifetime residual income!**

Yes, we just plug your people right into our training system, and the cycle begins again.

This is what you call a "Greased Chute". Step 1 flows smoothly into Step 2. Step 2 into Step 3. Step 3 into Step 4. Step 4 into Step 1.

And so on and so on.

The term "greased chute" means there are NO bumps along the way. No impediments, nothing whatsoever to even slightly slow the flow of a prospect from one step to the next.

To be long-term successful, you MUST have a "greased chute" marketing system for your opportunity. I love ours because it offers total training in the skills of working with people, so that you get better and better ... and your people can plug into exactly the same system, making it far easier for you to help them as you gain more & more experience.

#8
Paydirt!
Get And
Keep
Your
People

OK. I'm Not Tom Cruise.
But I'm Not Elmer Fudd, Either …

One day when I was 16, I was working in my dad's auto repair shop. A strikingly beautiful woman, mid-to-late 30s, walked in.

She took my breath away.

Curious, I looked into the lot to see what kind of car she drove.

'64 Ford Galaxy. Two-door. Turquoise.

And that wasn't all.

INSIDE the car was someone who looked a lot like her, only younger.

I was hypnotized. I had to get closer.

I did.

We talked for 15 minutes.

I came back into the shop, went in the office, shut the door, leaned against the wall, closed my eyes.

I pictured the day Linda & I would get married.

That was 36 years ago. She's still the love of my life. (Plus, I have the hottest mother-in-law you could EVER imagine!)

I knew it the instant I saw them.

What would you be willing to do to create that kind of impression on YOUR prospects?

The Dark Side of MLM

People figure they have a great company, great products, excellent marketing plan, good skills, proven track record, and on and on ... so success in this business should be like rolling off a log.

And then they get crushed UNDER the log!

Some facets of this business are so obvious, you may take them for granted ... and never actually DO them.

For instance.

We talked earlier about a huge, all-encompassing, powerful "WHY" that will keep you going in your business, no matter what you come up against.

But you need ANOTHER huge, all-encompassing, powerful "WHY".

THIS "WHY" is the reason your prospects should choose YOU over all their other 650 home business options. Your job is to make an impression on them that they will NEVER forget!

I don't know your business. I don't know what advantage YOU offer that puts you head and shoulders above your competition.

I only know that if you can't offer that kind of advantage,

You Are ROADKILL!!

You got NO chance.

So to help give you some ideas, I'll tell you the advantage we offer our prospects that elevates us above all the competition:

"I'll provide a lead generation system that brings ONLY the most qualified people into your group. Then I'll train them FREE, 5 nights a week, to build relationships and become Top Sponsors who will build YOU a lifetime residual income!"

… or the short version:

"I will personally help you get, mentor, and keep your people – for FREE, 5 nights a week!"

You are certainly welcome to become part of our group and use OUR advantage.

But in any event, you MUST be able to put YOUR focused advantage into a few words to create a lasting impression and elevate you above all your competition.

"So What?"

There's a very well-known Direct Marketing guy (See? I DO know some of them!) who once told me that after he writes an ad, he reads every sentence to himself and asks,

"So What?"

If he doesn't have a good answer, that sentence is GONE!

"So What?" is a good benchmark for YOU to use as you build your business. Everything you plan to do ... every sentence you write ... ask yourself, "So what?" In other words ...

Am I on-target?

Have I gotten hypnotized by a side-issue and gone off in some time-wasting direction?

Is this piece critical to the final picture?

Does this make sense? Can other people follow it?

"So what?" will help you execute.

You'll learn to be surgical in focusing on what's important.

You'll get rid of much of the clutter in your life.

It will help you define your competitive advantage.

I strongly recommend it.

Your Ex-Spouse Was An Optimist

OK. Listen. I'm NOT talking to you here. But just be still and listen in anyway.

See, I'm talking to the guy who downloaded this e-book right after you. HIS ex-spouse told him he probably was being a little unrealistic (not her exact words, but that's the gist) pinning his future financial hopes on a company that promised him:

- He wouldn't have to work - it would all be done for him.
- He wouldn't have to actually deal with and recruit any yucky people – his group would be built automatically through "spillover."
- He wouldn't have to sell – his people who spilled over would do that.
- He could get rich just by clicking his mouse.

And other than that, all he'd have to do is deposit the checks!

In fact, our boy's ex-spouse actually went so far as to imply that if a person is lazy, greedy & gullible, they

probably don't have a bright future in business.

She was right, of course. But that's only half the story.

In some cases, it's actually sincere people who make those offers, because they're so afraid nobody will join them if they know there's actual WORK involved. When you train people to do nothing but wait for you to do it for them, you wind up with people who do EXACTLY what you've trained them to do... nothing!

OK. Enough of that. It doesn't apply to YOU, anyway. Let's get on to the evaluation.

This formula has 5 parts. Each is important.

Here they are, in order of "easiest to evaluate."

It Just SEEMS Like Brain Surgery

People ask me all the time,

"Michael! What is the BEST compensation plan?

Here's my answer.

The best comp plan has 2 key features:

1. It works "with" the numbers (I'll get to these in a minute)

2. Average people (part-timers) can build & prosper. (The vast majority in your group will be average people).

Most network marketers are doomed from the get-go because the compensation plan they are working does not work with the numbers.

102

Don't listen to me. Just listen to the numbers.

I used to race dirt bikes. When 59 motorcycles come off a 27-foot high jump, not one single bike EVER "magically" floats up.

Fifty-nine out of 59 come crashing back to mother earth.

Gravity.

You cannot SEE gravity.

Makes no difference if you like gravity or not. Or if you understand it.

But if you jump motorcycles, you sure better learn to work with it.

In 26 years in network marketing, I've learned that you have to become a numbers-cruncher or die. You may not LIKE the numbers, you may not understand them.

Doesn't matter.

The numbers are reality.
Either work with them, or sayonara.

So ... what are the key network marketing numbers?

1. If you ask virtually any successful network marketer about their success, they'll tell you most of their income comes from 2 to 3 people in their group.

I'm not making up that number. I have learned to work with it.

2. MLM industry statistics tell you that "average" distributors sponsor 2.7 people into any home based business in their career.

I'm not making up that number. I have learned to work with it.

Do you see a connection between these two sets of numbers?

Yellows make up 35% of the population. They don't like aggressive people.

Blues make up 15% of the population. They don't like being sold.

Greens make up 35% of the population. They don't like pushy people.

Reds make up 15% of the population. One-third of Reds don't like being sold, either.

3. So 90% of the population, 9 people out of 10, 900 people out of 1000 don't like pushy, aggressive people, or being sold.

I'm not making up that number. I have learned to work with it.

When I call prospects I have 9 out of 10 people 900 people out of 1000 leaning forward wanting to find out, how I can help them reach their dreams.

This is because I lead with benefits, benefits, benefits,

I NEVER, never sell or close them.

People ask me all the time, "Michael, why do my people just SIT there? Why don't they DO something?"

Well, brand this MLM truism on your brain:

If you sell or close your people to join your opportunity, you will have to re-sell them every month to get them to do any work!

Logic & experience will tell you THAT statement is true.

So back to the compensation plan question. Just work with the numbers and you'll never go wrong.

If the "magic" number that most people sponsor is 3, then any plan wider then 3 will not work for the masses.

Note to the Red "Super Recruiters:" I know, I know. You can sponsor 3 people a day. Maybe 3 a minute.

The bad news is, you only make up about 3% of the population. Your best bet is a plan that pays you fast-start money on everyone you personally sponsor and that also pays leadership bonuses to infinity for unlimited income.

Best of Both Worlds

So my question is: Do you want a compensation plan that works for 97% of the people or a plan that works for 3%?

Another note: I'm pretty analytical when it comes to compensation plans. I LOVE a company that lets me personally sponsor someone, then place them ANYWHERE in my group to maximize THEIR dollar pay-out. You build trust & retention this way.

So my advice is, avoid any comp plan that:

1. Limits your strategy to place personally sponsored people where you want.
2. Forces you to go wide.
3. Doesn't reward you for building deep.
4. Won't work for average part-timers.

Remember: numbers are just like gravity. Work with them, not against them. Choose a compensation plan that works with the numbers and the masses.

Last One In Is a Rotten Egg

When the timing is right, NON-network marketers will take your product to the marketplace. The timing means NOW. Not 5 years earlier. Not 5 years later. I'll take timing over hard work every time.

Millionaires have been made in this industry JUST because of timing alone. Nothing else.

So how can you gauge the timing?

It's not easy, but here are some tips:

1. You'll waste a lot of time, money & energy getting in too early, because a large percentage of these companies fail in the first year or two.

2. You'll waste a lot of time, money & energy getting in too late. If the company is a household name (imagine the MLM companies you think of as dinosaurs), its momentum growth period occurred years ago. You're fighting a real uphill financial battle to start new in companies like this.

3. You want to get in AFTER a company has proven it has staying power (maybe 3-5 years), but BEFORE its

momentum growth period (in general, the time it takes a company to go from $100,000,000 to $500,000,000 a year). If you can find a company like this, and which also has the other parts of the formula in place, some fun work will give you the chance to ride a momentum wave to wealth.

Never Dedicate Your Life
To An Inanimate Object

In this industry if your product is not remarkable, you are invisible.

You need a product people will buy even with no compensation plan.

I get calls from people who tell me they're searching for a product that truly inspires them.

And that is exactly the wrong way to go about this.

What I tell them is to search to find a mob of people raving about a product ... THEN

Fall in Love With THAT Product!

Be a passionate advocate for it. Find a product with a HUGE market and fall in love with it.

Some people love to work for companies with a product that fits their self-image ... but they can't make a dime on it.

Do yourself a favor. Focus on the people. Focus on the market. Choose a product that everyone else wants.

And then, as you build your people, let them know the wisdom of doing the same thing.

A Whole Lotta Connivin' Goin' On

Every time we have ever seen a company or downline explode and go away, it does so because of the same 2 reasons: GREED and EGO.

True leaders are the Mentors with the servant's heart. It's never about the money. No Money Focus = No Greed. Build people and people will build the business.

People are people. They are not a number. They have goals, dreams & desires. Network marketing is not a sales business. Network marketing is a teaching & mentoring business. So the track record & attitude of leadership is important.

The simplest check you can do is to go to http://www.google.com , take the names of the leaders, stick them in quote marks ("name"), and search each name. If there are any big negatives about these people anywhere, they will probably come up in this search.

Opportunity Hides In The Tall Grass

You need a tested, proven, duplicatable success system. This has been well-described in the preceding 2 chapters.

Everyone you sponsor and everyone they sponsor needs a step by step system to get off to a fast start: online, offline, one on one, cold market, warm market, retailing, recruiting, becoming a mentor to their personally sponsored people. They don't need to do it all, but they need all those techniques available to them.

I feel pretty safe in saying you are never ever, EVER in this business going to find a company that provides you a realistic, useable, affordable system to do all the things you & your people will need to do.

But every company has individual groups of entrepreneurial reps who have put together such a system. THESE are the people you want to find and work with.

Don't join a group unless they have such a system in place.

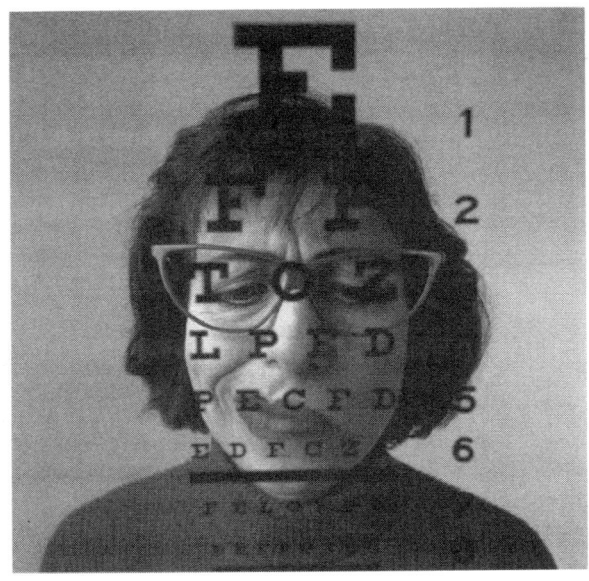

Multiple Streams of Outgo

The vast majority of network marketers who get convinced of the brilliance of the idea that they need multiple streams of income wind up instead with multiple streams of outgo.

Consider all the money-makers you've signed up for. Consider all the $$ you've paid for them. And consider the income they bring you right now, this month.

To borrow a line from Dr. Phil, "How's THAT working for you?"

There's a better way.

IBM was a 35-billion-dollar leader before anyone ever heard of Michael Dell.

Today? Dell swamps IBM in personal computer sales.

Why? Dell focused.

Assaulted Right & Left

The competition for your prospect's mind is fierce. The average mind gets

How can a 72-person FDA safety team monitor the effects of more than 13,000 prescription drugs on 200 million people with a budget of around $15 million a year?

* 9 hours of TV, radio, internet, newspapers, magazines, books, and videos a day.
* 40,000 words a day.
* 280,000 words a week.
* 14 million+ words a year.

To paraphrase a memorable line from Paul Newman's "Cool Hand Luke" movie of the late 1960s, "What we have here is a failure to STOP communicating!"

Overcommunication is rampant. To get through, you must focus to a pinpoint.

The narrower you focus, the better chance prospects & customers will see you as high quality. And NO SERIOUS BUILDER commits to a network unless they consider it high quality.

How To Send Prospects Racing For The Exit

When you promote a smorgasbord of opportunities, you undermine your network.

111

When you try to appeal to everybody with your multiple streams of products & services, smart people will not take you seriously. And why should they? You have no identity in their mind.

Result?

No trust. No loyalty. No network. Your people are easy targets for some narrowly focused networker.

You waste time & money searching for more opportunities to create your multiple streams. But loss of focus = loss of power.

You ruin your quality perception, because, to consumers, specializing = quality.

You're a mile wide and an inch deep. You're weak everywhere instead of strong somewhere.

You struggle to promote numerous unrelated products & services that you don't know well.

If you do establish a money-maker, you waste that profit on your other unsuccessful "streams of income."

You lose efficiency, competitiveness, and you get a smaller market share.

In my opinion, you are WAY better off to do your research, choose the RIGHT opportunity, and FOCUS ON THAT ONE!

Go Ahead – Argue With Me!

I can hear it now:

"You're wrong, Michael. These internet guys make a fortune, and they don't focus. They promote dozens, maybe HUNDREDS, of affiliate programs.'

So I've heard. Maybe it's true.

But my question is still, "How's that working for YOU?"

Given your skills, your knowledge, your time, your resources ... and most of all, your results so far ... are you better off focusing on one big profit center? Or are you better off sifting through (and spending money promoting) a ton of affiliate programs to find a few that work well?

Only YOU can answer that question.

How One Famous Company Drove Their Customers Away

Some years ago, Coca Cola sent this letter to restaurant owners across the U.S.:

"Has PepsiCo opened a restaurant near you yet? Wait 4 hours. Every 4 hours PepsiCo adds another unit to their restaurant empire. Another unit that competes with your business and feeds your customers."

In addition to selling colas, PepsiCo owns Pizza Hut, Taco Bell, & Kentucky Fried Chicken. If I owned a restaurant, the thought would never leave my mind that by stocking Pepsi, I'm subsidizing my competitors. So I would NEVER stock Pepsi.

The more streams of income you promote, the more chance you're competing with your own people. You see it every single day online.

No serious networker would risk alienating their people like this. You must scrupulously do your due diligence for anything you promote.

Ambushed By Human Nature & Common Sense

When you're splattered all over the universe, a mile wide and an inch deep, no one remembers your brand. Not customers, not prospects, not associates, not the media. Common sense tells them you're not quality. Human nature recognizes only a sharp, focused message.

On the other hand, your perfect focus attracts exactly the customers & associates you want. It excites them, because they're a part of something big. It tells them where they're going, inspires dedication and creates a belief in their minds that you'll be a big success.

It gives you power over all those "multiple streams of income" guys.

What Your Prospects Believe

- "The specialist knows more."
- "The better-quality product will win."
- "High price means high quality."
- "Low price means low quality."

So the easiest way to a quality perception in your prospect's mind is: "You can't have high quality AND low price. It's one or the other."

It's true most of the time. And it's certainly what your prospects believe. So the lesson is, "Focus on high quality." You can't go wrong.

The Sun, The Moon, The Stars, The Universe, & Your Prospect's Head

Your prospects have a ton of choices. How do they compare and evaluate?

It's tough. They talk about quality. But usually, they can't tell which is better. Opportunities, products, & testimonials look and sound similar.

So quality differences are hard to measure. But perception differences are real & measurable. If prospects perceive that you know exactly what you are doing, exactly where you are going, and that you care about their success, then you will get more than your share of people to work with.

Good people want to work with good people for a good company.

The finer your focus, the more power YOU will develop, because you will be perceived as ... and will become ... an expert. The cream of the crop.

To Thine Own Self Be True

Your #1 obligation is to stay in business, now and in the future. You do that by building your own web. And you do THAT by helping others build their own web.

Learn from the "multiple stream" guys. Those multiple streams stop any possible growth of a powerful, focused networking web. Most "income streams" lose money. There goes morale.

Specializing = Power.
A Focused Networker Builds a Focused Web

For example, we have staked out our ground. In our group, **we mentor people in person, and by phone, audiotape, & in writing, to build a marketing web by creating lifelong relationships.** That pinpoint specialty lets us dominate a very profitable segment of this industry.

You need to define your own focus, stake out your own ground.

Or, of course, you may want to join us. We'd love to have you.

In either case, a painful step that you MUST take is to define "who you are not."

Consider Rocket Chemical.

They were a 3-person company making aerospace lubricants. They developed an airplane anti-rust product which they named WD-40. Massive success followed. So Rocket phased out its other products and changed its name to WD-40 Company.

Result? They own "slippery" in consumer minds. Within a couple years, WD-40 was in 77% of American homes. Their net income hit 17% of sales, while the average Fortune 500 company net income is 5% of sales.

You need to be patient & brave. The market won't come overnight.

Think long-term. It's not, "Will this decision improve our numbers?" It's, "Will this decision improve our focus?"

I'll Get In Your Head & Under Your Skin

We are focused. We are the absolute leader in "Mentoring For Free" in the network marketing industry. We've been doing it for longer than I can remember. So we have expertise, results, & power that others will never have.

My goal is to own THAT piece of your mind.

We EXPECT to get the best people working with us. We EXPECT new people to call us, asking to join our group.

And, I'm proud to say, they do.

YOUR goal should be to focus on a niche that YOU can own in your prospect's mind.

Let's Get Illogical!

Focusing can be torture.

That "multiple streams of income" idea they all talk about sure is logical, isn't it?

Logic says the best way to improve your short-term income is to market MORE products & services. In other words, unfocus.

It's TOTALLY illogical to think that "To increase sales, narrow the focus."

But if it were logical, everyone would do it. You'd get no advantage.

Never Underestimate The Cost of Logic

A1 Steak sauce dominated its market. But people began eating more and more chicken. What to do?

They developed a new product: "A1 Poultry."

But in the customer's mind, A1 isn't a brand. It's the sauce itself.

Result? Despite an ad budget probably exponentially larger than ANY ad budget you or I will ever have in our wildest dreams, A1 Poultry flopped.

Multiple streams of income are incredibly risky for a long-time successful company that knows their market backwards and forwards.

For you and me? Good grief!

A Series of Harmless Decisions? HAH!

WARNING! When You Have These Thoughts,
You Are About To Create Multiple Streams of Outgo:

* "What else can I sell?"
* "This isn't happening fast enough. Let's speed it up. "
* "Some customers can't afford us. We need to add a cheaper product line."
* "We'll make more money if we offer these other products to that other market."
* "Our competition is REALLY tough. Let's do something else."
* "We need more variety so we'll sell more products."
* "All right! We did that good. Now, let's broaden our base."
* "How do we sell to our non-customers?"
* "WHAT? Let go of my other 'income streams'? Are you crazy?"
* "Let's just offer this new one along with the old one. Let the customer decide."

The "multiple streams of income" advice is one of the most logical things I've ever heard.

Only problem with it is, it doesn't work.

I hope you're strong enough to defy it.

Yum, Yum, Yum!

When you put your energy into one powerful income producer, your spin-off potential is tremendous.

The biggest problem for most people is focus ... the ability to do one thing amazingly well. I recommend you point all

119

your talents, knowledge, studying & training into creating a superb spiderweb business. On the back of THAT, you can spin-off in many directions (pun intended).

For instance ... I was mentored by Tom "Big Al" Schreiter. From Tom, I learned mentoring skills. I helped others. Through experience & study, I sharpened & improved my skills.

Today we have a large business, and mentoring for free makes it all possible.

It's tough to pick a niche - you have so many choices. Only focus gets you there. I highly recommend you start with a good, successful mentor of your own.

Of course, you could be terribly wrong when you first start. The amazing, wonderful thing you're doing can turn out to not be what you think it is. Yet you persist, while holding the day job.

We've certainly taken some risks. I don't recommend that for everyone. But, the scariness and risk helped us focus.

You can have your cake and eat it too. But first comes sacrifice. Then persistence. Then go to the cake store and eat all you want.

Yum, Yum, Yum!

Special New Bonus Section!

What I've learned in the 3 years since publication of the *"Success In 10 Steps"* ebook ...

Proof That It's Not Your Fault!
Discover How MLM "Opportunities" Stack The Deck Against You

The more you look at compensation plans and companies and company owners, the more you realize that the business model drives the behavior in the field.

This is why so many people fail in network marketing.

If the cards are stacked against you from the start, you won't be able to compete in the marketplace.

Business models drive behavior in the field

You may be in a company that drives unsuccessful behavior in the field. I don't want to hurt your feelings, or to tell you you've wasted months or years of your life. On the other hand, if I was struggling, I wish somebody thought enough of me to tell me why I can't get it going.

So how does the business model drive the behavior in the field? Think about this in a compensation plan.

Compensation Plan Breakage

Compensation Plan "Breakage" is money that, according to the comp plan, appears to go to the distributors. But for a variety of reasons, this money instead reverts back to the company itself. Here's a real scenario.

You have Companies A, B, & C. (These are real companies, but unnamed for obvious reasons.):

Company A – huge company, publicly traded.
Company B – also huge, as big as Company A, many years in the business, not publicly traded.
Company C – been around about 5 years, not nearly as big in dollar volume or in number of reps as A or B.

Let's look at the difference in business models of these companies, and the difference in behavior that these business models drive in the field, with regard to breakage.

First, let's agree on one point: if you check 20 successful, experienced, proven companies, all selling identical products with identical ingredients, you'll find their product wholesale cost is probably within pennies of each other

OK.

Companies A, B & C sell an identical amazing product.

Company A's version retails for $116.
Company B has the same product, at $104 retail.
Company C has the same product, at $40 retail.
Again those are all retail prices.

So what behavior is driven in the field with companies A & B? Do you think distributors can sell product at that price?

You'd probably agree, it would be a tough sell.

"Wow. There's a real problem with the business model."

Why? Because if I talk to 100 network marketers and ask, "Have you ever sold a product to your mother, father, best friend … at retail? Or do you always sell it to them at wholesale?" 99% of the time they say, "wholesale price."

Why? Because …

1. The product is too expensive.
2. They don't feel right making money off of mom & dad. They brought you into the world – just sell to them at wholesale, or give it to them.

Result? For companies A & B, there is NO retail activity going on, because the products are too expensive.

So … what behavior does that drive?

That's easy – sign up to be a distributor!

Company B is not publicly traded like Company A. But B's business model (set up in pre-internet days) was excellent personalized customer service.

Company C, formed just a few years ago, created an automated model without all the phone operators. About 97% their orders are placed online.

Result? Companies A & B have very high overhead. Personnel, training, salaries, benefits, workman's comp, etc., etc., run about $2 million a month.

Company B's product wholesale price is $80.

How can Company C retail the same product for $40? Much lower overhead.

Again, what happens in the field? A & B reps cannot retail product. So they resort to recruit, recruit, recruit.

Some new reps will always try to retail. But they soon realize their price is way too high. Consumers scoff. The reps lose interest – their heart isn't in it anymore, and they're gone.

In her book, ***If My Product's So Great, How Come I Can't Sell It?***, Kim Klaver says that when you talk to 100 targeted people, you'll get 10 retail sales and 1 distributor.

Now, Company A & Company B have overhead so high, they have to charge $80, where Company C is charging $40 for the identical product.

Does YOUR Company's Business Model Stop Retailing?

In Companies A & B, ordering online is complicated. Almost nobody does it. So both kept hiring order-takers.. Company B brags about their 400 employees answering the telephone and taking orders. What is the monthly cost of 400 employees? Let's say they're paying $10 an hour, plus social security, workman's comp, disability insurance, sick days, holidays … so it's really $20 an hour.

Managers probably get $20 an hour … double that to $40. They're in a building. Figure mortgage, power, phone, air conditioning, probably 200 computers, etc.

With more humans, you'll have more problems, so you'll need more customer service. You need more employees to fix the mess-ups of the humans.

Nice business model.

The Model That Encourages Retail Sales

Company C has a 95% online order system, plus a few operators who handle both customer service and customers who don't want to order online. You place the order online with your address and credit card info. Fewer mistakes, so you don't need as many customer service people.

Company A and Company B have sky-high overhead, but here's what they say: "Our price is $80 because our product is the best. Rare and expensive blind leprechauns harvest the mold off the rock every other full moon."

Or it's their superduper special ingredient that no one else has. They have to say something to convince the distributor base that the $80 price is actually a good value.

If You Can't Retail, What's Left?

Is this model clear? Do you understand why Company A & Company B have such a hard time selling that product?

So this business model drives behavior in the field of recruit, recruit, recruit. *But Company C, with the latest technology, doesn't have nearly the overhead.* So they sell the identical product for half the price.

Companies A & B can't get customers, so they have to recruit distributors. So people have to pay money to

become a distributor to then buy the product for $80, the wholesale price. But ... is that a fair price?

The Greatest Irony of "Recruit v. Retail"

When you sell a great product, you wind up with a certain percentage of people who absolutely love the product. They become dedicated consumers. They'll never be without that product. And some percentage become reps.

But when you just recruit, THAT dedication is not there. You'll certainly keep some of your recruits. But many will continue looking. Once they find a better deal, they're gone. This rarely happens with a dedicated product user. So retailing product gives a whole new dynamic to your business that most MLMers don't have.

What Network Marketers Can Learn From The Walmart Business Model

What is the lifeblood of ANY business?

Product movement to the end consumer. Have you read Sam Walton's autobiography? His vision, the business model he pioneered, was brilliant. Walton started Walmart & Sam's Club. He said, "We will be the largest retailer in the world." And he achieved this goal because he found a way to move product to the end consumer at the cheapest price. How did he do that?

Walton said, "Do people care when they buy their groceries whether there's an acoustical tile ceiling, or if they see roof rafters and white bar joists?" The answer: They don't care. So he invented a business model where you have shelves with cases and cases and cases of soda pop.

In the evening, they bring that stuff down & fill the shelves. They stock the warehouse for ALL the manufacturing companies, saving those companies a TON of money.

He built massive warehouses around the world. Then he talked to Scott Tissues, Hershey's, Johnson & Johnson, Levi's, all these companies: "Hey! Don't build expensive warehouses all over the place. Ship your products to MY warehouses, I'll store it. As we sell it, I'll pay you."

So when they scan that bar code, Scott Tissues knows Walmart sold 73 cases of paper towels today. The system tracks that sale. At the end of each day, Walmart sends each vendor the money.

Everybody Else Became An "Also-Ran"

Other retail outlets don't have the space – or the vision – to make that offer to suppliers. Instead, they buy the stuff in smaller quantity, store it in the back, and move it to the front as needed. There's no tall, tall, tall ceiling with products stacked way up above you. That's the way it's always been done. But that's not how Walmart does it.

Why Customers Choose Walmart

So Walmart & Sam's Club pay less for identical products than other retail outlets. And they can pass the savings on to consumers, attracting throngs of buyers to their stores.

does Sam Walton make money with Sam's Club? Off the membership. Again, that and the warehousing of products allow them to sell at a very low price. It's in the business model. Whoever figures how to move product to consumers at the best price, wins. Sam Walton proved that point.

How did he do it? **He cut the overhead for all those companies, his product suppliers!**

How does this apply in network marketing? Look at every company, every compensation plan. Let's say every company pays out 50% of retail to reps. Each product, no matter the cost, they pay 50% commission.

You can only cut the pie so many ways. If you pay 50% commission on $79.95, or 50% commission on the identical product at $39.95. Do you think a $39.95 product makes it much easier to sell twice as much or 3 times as much?

Cut the overhead, and you have a better chance to sell that product. You're not just competing against other network marketing products. You're competing against Sam's Club & Walmart, too. Your business model better let you make a good offer to the consumer, or you'll never succeed.

Whatever network marketing company finds a way to move the product to the end consumer at the best price, wins.

The Problem With The "Catalog" Business Model

It's been a trend in network marketing for the last 5 years to sell a single product. Here's why.

Some companies started getting 200, 300, 400 products. With that many products, people get confused. Send somebody to a website with 100 products and they go "Uh-h-h-h ... omigosh!" They don't order anything.

What Drives The "Beautiful Website" Business Model?

Network marketing companies design a website promoting some big, beautiful, fancy building somewhere, talking about how great the company president is, etc.

You want to buy a product, but you can't find it. Why? *Because they're shoving the business opportunity down your throat.* Of every 100 people, 89 don't care, 10 are more interested in product, 1 is more interested in the business opportunity. So why would you feature the business opportunity and hide the product?

Because the product is too expensive, and you know no one will buy it without a bizop attached!

Websites That Work?

Network marketing companies tell you that you can't design your own website. They need to choose their top 2 or 3 products and showcase each of them on an individual website. So if I drive traffic to the site for Product X, Y, or Z, there is NO mention of a business opportunity.

Again, 90% of people don't want the business opportunity. They just want to buy a product. But the company says, "No, no, no. Get them in the deal, get them in the deal."

Wrong message. You're working against the numbers, and that will kill you. If 10 out of 100 just want product, and you say, "Nope. You gotta join, or no product!" ... can you imagine why you're not having success?

The Problem With The "Single Product" Business Model

Many new MLMs sell just one product. They have big growth for a 1-3 years, and then they flatline. Why?

The most expensive thing you'll ever do is get that new customer. Let's say I promote a phone company. You sign up for my long distance service. If I'm your phone guy, then I also need to be your cell phone guy, your DSL guy, your local service guy. I need to be THE phone guy.

As a customer, you'll buy 4, 5, 6 products from me. And if I've got those 6 products, I can probably bundle them to you cheaper than you could ever go buy them individually.

If a person drinks a health beverage, aren't they also likely to want something to take care of their digestive system? Don't they need vitamins? Don't they want something to bolster their immune system, keep from getting sick? If they have aches & pains, don't they buy something to help?

If they aren't buying all that with YOUR company, they're getting it somewhere else. Maybe you sell a vision plan. It's a benefits plan, you better have a legal plan, a dental plan, more services they can use. If you don't provide those services, they'll get them somewhere else.

The "Hybrid" Business Model

The idea is to have other products for the back-end. The person has been using your feature product. You've built know, like & trust with them. And suddenly they say, "Ohmigosh! They have other products here. I use these anyway. I can just buy them all here."

What behavior is created in the field if you have just a single product? You, work, work, work … and you burn through the market. Every professional marketer knows you have to sell more products to the same customer.

The Tested, Proven, Winning
Online Business Model

When you spend your time or your money or both to drive traffic to a website, take advantage of the traffic. You need a lead capture page, where you offer some valuable freebie to people in exchange for their contact information. That way, you have a real person you can start building a relationship with. Network marketing is a relationship business, not a sales business.

A lady told me that pay-per-click search engines don't work. She spent $10 and got 170 people to click through to her company website, and none joined her business!

I'll bet if she got 17,000 people to click through, none would join her business. You must build "know, like, & trust." Offer them some valuable freebie in exchange for their contact information. That's exactly the system we give you at MentoringForFree.com.

Sending traffic to your company website is 100% a waste of time & money, unless that website is a carefully designed lead capture page. That is the tested, proven, winning business model on the internet. Violate that business model at your own peril.

So you're in a network marketing company, and you send traffic to your website. I want to buy a single product. I go to

131

your website, and you tell me about the company president and how great she is, you've got a brand-new building, you're debt-free, and all that stuff. You just jam the business opportunity down my throat.

Can you see how that drives away potential customers?

Create Your Own Lead Capture Page? Uh-Oh …

What if you create your own product page? You've violated the Policies & Procedures, because your page has to be approved by corporate. You have to ask permission.

And the company's business model is "recruit, recruit, recruit." So their pages are about "recruit," not retailing product. In the real world, if Kim Klaver is right – and I truly believe she is, because I see it in my business – then of 100 prospects, 10 would be customers & 1 would be a distributor.

If you create product sales, you'd need fewer people sponsored to make a bigger check.

This Is Why You Must Start In The Right Place

So it's critical to put yourself in the right position, with the right company, from the start. Otherwise, you'll pedal and pedal and pedal and pedal and pedal and pedal … and you'll never get anywhere. You'll burn yourself out.

And for many people, that is the end of them in this business. They just decide it doesn't work.

If you're in the right company, with a good opportunity, good commission numbers, your position is right, and you have an idea how to market, then it can work for you quickly. Otherwise, you have problems.

Smart Companies Understand Leverage

Back to Sam Walton. Every store sells Scott Tissues™. But Sam Walton warehoused the product, and he didn't charge the suppliers for that. They actually loan him the product until he sells it. Then he pays them for it the next day.

So Walmart doesn't lay out money to buy product. It's Scott Tissue's™ money. Walmart actually uses their suppliers' money to stock product! Brilliant! They didn't pay for product up front, and their business model moves product to the end consumer at the cheapest price.

People say, "Yes, but Walmart's got cheap stuff."

Ok. But it's the same stuff you buy at the other stores ... where you pay more! It's made by the same manufacturer. Walmart just cut the overhead, so you pay less.

So you always need to look at business models and the behavior they drive in the field.

"We're Better, Because We Have Our Own Lear Jet!"

We've talked about compensation plans and how the overhead is built into the breakage. So the more frugal your company is ... you know, people tell me, "Well, our company, the president has a jet!" Man, I don't want to hear that the company has a jet! That's your overhead. It comes out of your commission!

Don't tell me your company President wears alligator skin boots. That's nuts. I don't want to know that he's got 4 or 5 assistants to get him through the day. That is all overhead.

YOU WIN when you find the company that moves product to the end consumer at the best price. THAT is the winning business model. Use that as your guide. Then start looking.

You want a comp plan that pays you on volume, minimal or low volume for retailing a product … and I'm not talking about a company promoting their wholesale & retail price and telling people to sell it at retail & collect the difference. That never happens in MLM. It's a smoke & mirrors word game, we all know that. Nobody actually does it.

The Famous "70% Rule" And Other Loser Mumbo-Jumbo

So if that's the reality, look at the Policies & Procedures. They talk about **The 70% rule**. In other words, they don't want you stockpiling product to qualify for a bonus check. So they will talk and talk and talk about The 70% Rule, which says you are supposed to sell or consume 70% of each order before you place your next order. So they're making sure you aren't stockpiling.

And the company that has no retail activity will spend 3 or 4 paragraphs talking about the 70% rule. A company with good retail activity will hardly even mention it, because it's just not an issue.

If a company always sells its products at the retail price, and it's a value price, you'd never have to waste your time talking about the 70% rule. Those products would get consumed, everybody would pay retail.

But that's not the case. A company will say, "Well, this product sells for $104. But if you become a distributor, you can buy it at the super-low price of $79.95!" And that extra $24 is the breakage from the company.

If The Business Model Doesn't Fit Your Personality, You Will Fail

OK. I think we have a very clear picture of breakage and compensation plans and what behavior that drives. Now, let's look at a compensation plan against a personality type.

Let's say you're a Yellow personality, the loving, giving, caring, nurturing person. You want to work deep, deep, deep in your organization, to help people. And your company has a stairstep-breakaway compensation plan. Let's say it's $1,000, $2,000, $3,000, $4,000, $5,000 … increments like that.

For the amazing closer – the one who can sell ice to an Eskimo – that $3,000 or $5,000 package is nothing. They'll sell those all day long, because they are a salesperson.

But Yellow – the nurturer – they can't even ask the person for the money because they're thinking, "Ohmigosh, that's a lot of money. If they don't sell this stuff, they'll have a lot of debt on their credit card. I don't want to be responsible for putting debt on their card. Oh no oh no oh no!"

That's what is going on in their head when they're talking to the prospect. So if you are a Yellow and you get into the sales arena with the Red, you will lose every time.

So here's the other business model: MLM compensation plans are designed for certain personality Colors! A stairstep-breakaway plan will never work for the Yellow. NEVER ... because it goes against them.

Several years ago we met a lady coming up on retirement. She'd spent 5 or 6 years trying to build a network marketing downline. She was a Yellow. Schoolteacher, nurturing, caring, late '50s or early '60s. She had tried 3 different MLM companies, and all 3 had stairstep-breakaway compensation plans. It was amazing!

She struggled to build a business that went against her personality. She switched companies to a compensation plan that suited the Yellow personality, and suddenly, she had success. Within 2 years, she was full-time, debt-free.

So again, the business model only works for certain personalities. If you're not having success in network marketing, you need to figure out your personality type – get **Powerful Networking Secrets** or the **Color To Success** CD. Read the ebook, listen to the CD, figure out your personality, then get some coaching or mentoring on "Does this compensation plan work for YOU?"

No matter what you're selling, a product or service, you've got to see what is happening in the field in real time, in the real world.

The Business Model Dictates How You Can Successfully Do The Business

Then you can determine how to do the business. Is it about recruiting? Then you better get out there and recruit. If the plan doesn't pay you to retail, then go recruit. In any event, you need to ask yourself Kim Klaver's question: "If my product's so great, how come I can't sell it?"

So, if you're faced with THAT dilemma, then you need to make a change. Let's say you're in a binary compensation plan. You have a left leg and a right leg. If you bought product through the binary plan, it would pay you, ordinarily, another 5 – 7 %.

So is there any incentive at all, whatsoever, at any time, for me to ever retail product?

No matter how you do business, there is a fixed cost attached to each customer you get. Many direct marketers build huge businesses & incomes with consumable products when they can simply break even on the first order. They make their money on the re-orders. That is a very workable business plan.

And however they advertise and get that original customer, they'll usually spend a minimum of 35% of the cost of the product, and even up to 100%, just to get that new customer. So if you are paid 7% to sell a product, that tells you right there that this company has absolutely no inten-tion of anyone actually retailing product. You'd go broke trying to do that, and it would never be profitable for you.

So experienced marketers wouldn't go near any product that paid less than, say, at least 25% per sale. If you retail a product, no matter what you're selling, you've got to look at about 25% commission as the bottom line. And if a company isn't paying that much, then you won't find any retailing going on., except by people who don't know what they're doing. And they won't be doing it long.

So know that going in. Those are the real numbers, the real world numbers. Plain and simple. Look at the business model, what behavior does it drive in the field? It's called recruit, recruit, recruit.

On the other hand, if you're getting 40% ... you start your marketing on a small scale, testing & measuring everything, tweaking it until you've got it right. But Holy mackerel! Once you've got it right, you can do it for a long, long time, roll it out, and make a ton of money!

Business model compensation plans drive the behavior in the field. All you have to do is look at the business model to know the future of this company and whether it'll be easy to do, or hard to do, or totally impossible. You'll know if there is a fit for you in there.

If you are that great salesperson, great recruiter, go-go-go-go-go, then you will get the best results in a certain pay plan ... like the stairstep breakaway, or the Aussie 2-up. If you're not that person, if you're in the other 92% of the world's population, and you don't like to sell or be sold, then you need to work some other pay plan.

If you stick with those hard-driving salespeople, they will tell you you're a failure, that it's your fault you aren't building, that you aren't working hard enough, you didn't make enough dials.

But the fact is, it just doesn't work.

Hopefully, this gives you a snapshot of just what to look for, so you see what's happening in the real world, and you can realize, it's not your fault. The company designed it that way. They've designed breakage in there, to benefit themselves. You're forced to treat people as a number, when that's not at all the way you feel. And that's why you struggle to build your business.

If you put yourself in the wrong place from the get-go, what chance do you have? NONE!

Again, breakage is the difference between the company's hard cost of product, and what they actually sell it for. For instance, you could say, "To get this 2% leadership bonus, you have to have $100,000 in volume down 4 legs, $25,000 each." So you could have $75,000 down one leg, but it only counts for $25,000. So they promote their 2% leadership bonus on all volume – but not all volume counts.

So much of the breakage is in the plan's fine print, the qualifications for you to actually get a check. You need to plug in real numbers into those qualifications they list for you to get paid, to figure out the breakage on each plan.

Red can be extremely successful in a stairstep breakaway plan. Yellows? No way. If you're in that stairstep plan, just target Reds.

This is how a plan creates retailing or recruiting, just by the business model.

Now ... if a company's overhead is too high, their prices won't be competitive. Twenty years ago, this company was very competitive. But computers & the internet changed the landscape. This company hasn't changed with them. They should have gone more computer, less hiring people. They didn't, and the distributors pay for that mistake.

Your Success Depends a LOT on Company Management Experience

When you have company management that has never been in network marketing, never built a downline, then how can you expect them to understand the business model? Many come from a Fortune 500 background, and that's the approach they use. It makes perfect sense … but it doesn't work in network marketing. Now they're locked in, and they have a huge problem.

The sad part is, many, many, many distributors, tens & hundreds of thousands of people, will join those opportunities and wind up wondering, "What's wrong with me? What am I doing wrong? I must be too tall. Too short. Too fat. Too skinny. I must be a loser."

Your company leadership has to have their ear to the ground, be aware of new technology, be willing to try new things. I consulted for a company a few years ago. They had a problem retaining customers. I told them they had to create a Customer Service Department that calls your customers and gets them to sample your product. It was actually a service, so it was crucial that they get customers to experience the service. It's amazing how many people sign up for stuff and never actually use it.

So in the field, reps were building, recruiting, selling, going and going. But the retail sale only stayed on the books 90 days. Yet the company was advertising they had 90% customer retention. Guess how they do it?

Let's say you sponsor me as a customer, and in 90 days, I don't want the service anymore. So the company sends YOU a letter and says, "Michael stopped being a customer. You need to talk to him and get him back. We'll give you 4 weeks to get him back. If you don't get him back, we will go after him, and then he will become our customer."

Ain't that a kick in the pants!

No wonder they 90% retention. When my customers drop off, the company no longer needs to pay me a commission. So they can give the customer a much cheaper service.

They're in competition with the distributors!

Comparing MLM To Other Business Models

A good buddy of mine sent me some stats. Some guy wrote a report that says 60% of the people who join MLM never make any money.

My friend did some research. Real estate agents spend about $1000 to go to school, plus $250-$500 for a license. And 60% quit without ever selling a single home.

Life insurance agents spend months in on-the-job training and must pass an exam in most states. More than 60% only sell ONE life insurance policy, and that is to themselves.

Three mortgage brokers who employ loan officers told me that after months of study, on-the-job training, and taking the test, 70-80% of loan officers drop out without ever earning a commission.

A friend of mine ran Kirby vacuum crews. After weeks of training, the dropout rate was 90% in the first 2 weeks.

Eighty to 90% of new car salespeople drop out without ever making a sale. Call your local car dealer.

So in just about any sales field, 60% or more drop out. And just about the same number of people drop out of college their freshman year, after spending $5,000 - $10,000 of Mom & Dad's money. A friend of mine sent his daughter to medical transcription school for $2,500 and 3 months of her life. She transcribed 10 tapes.

As they say, if it was easy, everybody would do it. Most people will ALWAYS fail, whether it's MLM, real estate, life insurance, door-to-door sales, or even going to college.

The key is to understand the landscape so you can put youself in the best position to be successful. You can have a realistic chance for MLM success if you understand what features you should look for in an MLM company.

Linda and I hope this book helps you in some way to reach your next level in network marketing. To learn how YOU can become the person you need to be to attract people to you, contact the person who gave you this book. Our FREE mentoring phone calls will give you all the specific details you need for success, and your friend who gave you this book has the times & phone number for those calls.

Sincerely,

Michael Dlouhy

Michael Dlouhy

PS: We do want you to know that we have a leads call where 90% of the people we call tell us, "Yes, I want to make additional income from home." To learn more about this call and our Free mentoring call, contact your source on the inside back cover of this book.